D

Martin Gostelow

JPM GUIDES

CONTENTS

unspoiled nature

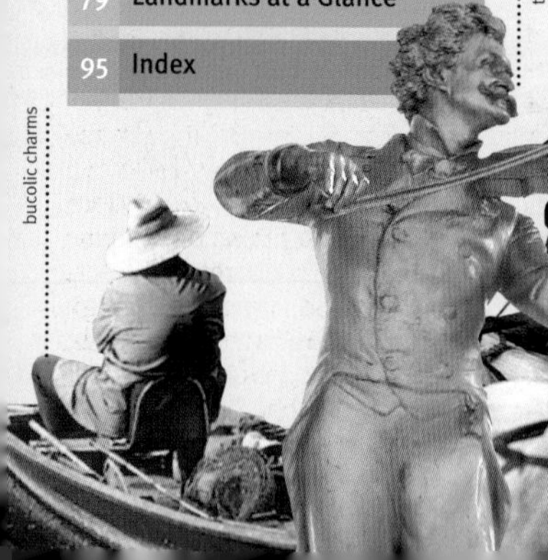

a pride in traditions

the sound of music

bucolic charms

ALONG THE DANUBE

Who can hear the name Danube without thinking of that most famous of Strauss waltzes: "On the Beautiful Blue Danube"? Beautiful it certainly is, but to be honest, it's more a brownish yellow than blue, thanks to the lime and mud stirred up from the river bed. The Danube's romance lies in the medieval castles, baroque churches and rococo palaces it passes on its way through central Europe and the Balkans, as well as the historic cities that have grown up along its banks.

International River

The great waterway begins in southwest Germany at the confluence of the Brege and the Brigach, and flows through eight other countries to the sea: Austria, Slovakia, Hungary, Croatia, Serbia, Romania, Bulgaria and Ukraine. Over a stretch of just 570 m, the Danube also flows through Moldova, making it another member of the International Danube Commission. Its 2,860 km (1,780 miles) make it Europe's second longest river, after the Volga. Barge traffic starts at the cathedral town of Ulm, larger vessels at Regensburg. Today, completion of the Main–Danube Canal extends navigation from the North Sea to the Black Sea, more than 3,200 km (2,000 miles).

Through Austria and Hungary

The Danube crosses from Germany into Austria at Passau, established as a frontier town by the Romans. It flows through the major port town of Linz to the Habsburgs' grand imperial city of Vienna. From Slovakia's capital, Bratislava, the river follows the Hungarian border until it makes a dramatic 90-degree turn at the Danube Bend and heads south to the Hungarian capital of Budapest. Here, it cleaves through the city, separating the old hill town of Buda from the more modern and much flatter Pest. Beyond the suburbs, the river returns to its bucolic mood, flowing through flat and fertile countryside. In all, the Danube's passage through Hungary stretches for 417 km (260 miles).

Borderline

From Budapest to the Black Sea, the river has regularly acted as a border, often separating rival kingdoms—or bitter enemies. Roman sentries and Dacian warriors kept watch on each other across the lower Danube; centuries later the armies of the Habsburgs faced the Ottoman Turks. Many of the towns were founded in Roman times, and medieval fortresses, castle ruins and memorials still attest to the battles which were fought here. Under the Austro-Hungarian Monarchy (1683–1918), the countries on the middle and lower reaches seemed to be united—the first and only time that a "Confederation of the Danube" has been a reality.

What's in a Name? The Donau in Germany and Austria, Duna in Hungary, Dunav to the Serbs, the Croats and the Bulgarians, Dunaj in Slovakia and Dunărea in Romania, the Danube was known as Istros to the ancient Greeks—and is Tuna to the Turks. The name derived from the Latin Danubius, the name of a Roman river god. However, its roots are far older, either from the Celtic or perhaps the Farsi *Danu*, meaning quite simply "to flow" or "to run". This ancient term is at the base of several other European rivers—the Donetsk, the Dniepr, the Don in Russia, and also the English River Don.

Tributaries

On its way to the Black Sea, the river passes through a succession of incredibly varied landscapes. In the Great Hungarian Plain (Nagy Alföld) it is joined by major tributaries: the Drava, the Tisza and the Sava. In those sections of the Danube with a very slight drop, such as along the Slovak-Hungarian border, in southern Hungary and northern Croatia, flood-plains are inundated year after year. The flooding has produced a remarkable zone of woods, ponds and streams, now protected as nature reserves and national parks, offering a refuge for richly diversified wildlife.

Iron Gate

The Danube achieves its greatest breadth below Belgrade. Further south, spectacular scenery awaits the voyager, as the river carves a cleft through the Southern Carpathian Mountains at the narrow gorge of the Iron Gate. A hydroelectric power plant was built here in 1971, making a major impact on the natural environment, but at least one positive result was that this stretch of the river, previously feared for its cataracts, became navigable for ships.

From the Iron Gate, the river flows into the lowlands of Walachia, where it is hemmed in on the Bulgarian side by craggy mountain spurs, whilst the opposite, Romanian bank is flat and marshy. The Danube turns northward before reaching the Dobrogea tableland, to turn back eastward at Galaţi. After this final dogleg, the marshy delta region begins.

The People

The Danubian region is a mosaic of diverse peoples. Today's Romanians are proud to claim Dacians and Romans as their ancestors; those of the Bulgarians were Slavs and Thracians. Germans, too, have had an impact on the culture of the region: in the 12th century, King Géza of Hungary brought Saxons into Transylvania, and in the 18th century Archduchess Maria Theresa of Austria settled Swabians on the lower Danube to revitalize and cultivate deserted lands. The political upheavals of the 20th century forced the majority of the descendants of these settlers to return to their former homeland.

Huber/Schmid

istockphoto.com/ene

istockphoto.com/Rus

The source of the Danube in the castle park of Donaueschingen. | A painterly view of Stein on the bank of the Danube. | The imposing Chain Bridge in Budapest. | Waterlilies in bloom.

Passau was built at the confluence of the Inn, the Danube and the Ilz.

FLASHBACK

About 250,000 years ago, *Homo palaeohungaricus*, a primitive form of human being, settled in the middle Danube valley, now Hungary, attracted by the abundance of water and wildlife, and perhaps even by the hot springs that remain a magnet to this day.

Trade along the Danube developed as far back as the Neolithic period (ca. 6000 BC). The Thracians, the original inhabitants of what is now Bulgaria, spread to the lands between the lower Danube and the northern Aegean around 1000 BC. By the 7th century BC, Greek sailors reached the Danube delta and explored upstream, opening the way for commerce.

Celtic tribes established themselves in the valley of the upper Danube, now southern Germany, by 600 BC. They spread eastwards, settling along the middle Danube and its tributary the Sava, and in the 3rd century BC built a fortress on the site of the future Belgrade. Under pressure from the Romans, Germanic tribes from northern Europe and the Iranian-descended Sarmatians, Celtic domination was broken by around 120 BC. In present-day Romania, the Dacian kingdom was born.

Rome Moves In

From 27 BC, under Emperor Augustus, the Romans' conquest of the Danube valley made the river they called the Danubius (and in its lower reaches, the Ister) the empire's northern border. On the other side lived a variety of tribal peoples the Romans labelled barbarians, among them Celts, Pannonians and Illyrians. A line of fortifications (Limes) was built along the river to repel barbarian incursions. Some 20,000 Roman soldiers were deployed between Vienna and Budapest, and still more along the upper and lower reaches of the river. A Roman fleet patrolled its waters and strongholds were constructed at strategic points on its banks. These quickly grew into flourishing towns, including Castra Regina (Regensburg), Vindobona (Vienna), Aquincum (Budapest), Singidunum (Belgrade) and Sexantaprista (Ruse). Other important riverside fortresses such as

Ratiaria (Vidin) and Nicopolis ad Istrum (Nikopol) were built at the mouths of tributaries.

In AD 106, the expansionist Emperor Trajan defeated the Dacians and so gained control of the entire course of the Danube, as well as extensive lands to the north, roughly the area now covered by Romania and Moldova. His successor Hadrian called a halt to further conquest, in order to concentrate on organizing and defending the vast territories under Roman rule.

In the 3rd century, Goths hailing from north of the Black Sea penetrated southwards to the Danube and crossed it in force. It took a strong Roman army led by the Emperor Gallienus and two future emperors, Claudius II and Aurelian, to defeat them at the battle of Naissus (now Nis in Serbia) in 269. The victory was so complete that it was almost a century before the frontier once again had to be defended against Goths and Sarmatians. Major invasions took place but also relatively peaceful immigration, in which whole tribes fleeing the warlike Huns were allowed to settle within the Empire.

Barbarians and Christians

In the 4th and early 5th centuries, large tribes of Goths and other Germanic peoples moved into the Danubian region and weakened the Roman Empire. Worse was to follow in the 5th century when Huns from the Asian steppes, led by Attila, ravaged southeastern Europe and invaded the Roman heartland of Italy itself.

In the 6th and 7th centuries, the previously little-known Slavs from eastern Europe expanded west and southwards, and in the lands which today form Bulgaria they intermingled with the Thracian population. In the 8th century Charlemagne, Emperor of the Franks, brought much of western and central Europe under his rule, driving out the Goths and the descendants of Attila's Huns. However, Magyars from somewhere between the Volga river and the Ural mountains settled in Hungary along with a lesser number of Turkic Petchenegs.

In the 10th century ten tribes—seven Hungarian Magyars and three Khazar—united to defend themselves from menacing Petchenegs, Russians and Bulgars. Prince Arpád, head of the Magyars, was named supreme leader. Hungary's conversion to Christianity in 975, initiated under a great-grandson of Arpád, Prince Géza, made the Danube a relatively safe overland route for pilgrims going to the Holy Land. Géza's son Stephen was crowned in the year 1000 as the first king of Hungary. Canonized after his death, Stephen became the country's patron saint. The river proved rather more perilous for the huge, disorganized groups of French and Germans who set out in 1096 on the so-called People's Crusade to "save" Jerusalem from Islam. Pillaging their way through Austria and Hungary, they soon antagonized the local people and there were many skirmishes and some full-scale battles. Later crusades however brought something of an economic a boom to the towns along the banks of the Danube. England's King Richard I the Lion-Heart was imprisoned in Dürnstein Castle on his way home from Palestine in 1192. In 1396, in the so-called "Last Crusade", an army of 100,000 Germans, French, Hungarians, Poles, Bohemians, Italians and Spaniards congregated at Budapest and advanced down the Danube—to meet with a crushing defeat by the Turks at Nicopolis, now Nikopol in Bulgaria.

The Viceroy of Hungary, János (John) Hunyadi, repelled Turkish invaders (1456) at Nándorfehérvár (now Belgrade) but died, probably of the plague, in the same year. His eldest son was murdered soon afterwards and his second son Mátyás (Matthias) was chosen by the Hungarian nobles to succeed as king at the age of 15. Renowned as the "just king" Matthias I Corvinus, he reigned from 1458 to 1490, regarded in Hungary as an intellectual golden age.

istockphoto.com/Palis

The spectacular ruins of Devín Castle in Slovakia near the border with Austria.

The Turkish Tide

In the 16th century, the Danube became the route of a "crusade" in reverse, as Suleiman the Magnificent's Ottoman Turks carried Islam west from the Black Sea. After the battle of Mohács in 1526, Hungary fell to the Ottomans for 150 years. Serbia, Bosnia and parts of Romania also came under their rule. However,

istockphoto.com/Moisei

An Orthodox icon in a church in Constanţa (Romania).

in spite of besieging it in 1529 and again in 1683, the Ottomans failed to take Vienna, which became the base for Austria's Habsburg rulers to undertake the gradual reconquest of Hungary by 1687, followed by Transylvania in 1691. The Treaty of Karlowitz (Sremski Karlovci) ended the war against the Turks in 1699 and made Austria the major power in the Danube region.

During the reign of Maria Theresa (1740–80), the peoples of most of the Danube region were united. The Archduchess moved German settlers into the areas that had been left deserted after the expulsion of the Turks, and these energetic newcomers introduced new methods of agriculture, developed trade and industry and built whole new villages and towns. The Ottoman Turks were not yet completely beaten; they still held large parts of the Balkans. However, in the Russo-Turkish War of 1768–74 Russia occupied the principalities of Moldavia and Walachia, and thanks to the Treaty of Svištov (1791), Austria gained the Iron Gate pass on the Danube near Orşova. Russia conducted further wars against Turkey, some of them in the Danubian region. In the Treaty of Adrianople (Edirne) in 1829, almost all of the Danube delta was ceded to Russia.

Another important event took place in 1829: the founding of the Donau-Dampfschifffahrtsgesellschaft (Danube Steamship Company). Its operations began with a service linking Vienna and Budapest. Until World War I it was the biggest inland shipping company in the world. Under the terms of the Treaty of Paris (1856) following the Crimean War, Russia lost control of shipping on the lower Danube, which was declared open to international traffic.

In 1877 the Russian Tsar Alexander II launched another war against the Turks, with the declared aim of freeing Bulgaria from their rule. After a five month-long siege and huge loss of life on both sides, the Turkish stronghold of Pleven fell to Russian forces, and in 1878 Bulgaria became an independent state. After 1870 the Danube was rerouted around Vienna to prevent flooding.

The End of an Empire

When World War I came to an end in 1918, the Austro-Hungarian monarchy collapsed; Hungary and Czechoslovakia became independent states, and the new Kingdom of the Serbs, Croats and Slovenes (later to be known as Yugoslavia) united a large part of the Balkans. An international Danube Commission was set up in 1923 to control traffic on the river from Ulm in southern Germany all the way to the Black Sea, and keep navigational equipment in good repair. In 1932 at a conference on Danubian affairs held in London, the French prime minister Tardieu even suggested an economic union of the nations of the Danubian region (although Germany was excluded), a forerunner of the European Union, but his plan failed to gain enough support. (In 1948, seven countries bordering the river revived the Danube Commission, which today has eleven member states.)

World War II and After

During World War II, the Danube became a battle line. German naval forces used the river to reach the Black Sea. The victorious Soviet army occupied Hungary and Romania in 1944 and marched into Belgrade, although Tito's partisans could take some of the credit for the defeat of the Germans.

In the aftermath of the war, communist regimes were imposed on the nations of Central Europe and the Balkans. Austria was divided into Soviet and western-controlled zones until 1955, when a peace agreement restored its independence as a neutral nation.

The fall of the Berlin Wall in 1989 has had far-reaching consequences for all the nations on the middle and lower Danube. The former Soviet-bloc states threw off the communist yoke, and most managed the transition to some form of democracy. The sad exception was Yugoslavia, where nationalist, ethnic and religious tensions led to its break-up. In 1999, Serbia, the largest of the six separate states that emerged from the wreck, launched an attack on its rebellious province of Kosovo, in defiance of international warnings. In response, NATO forces bombed the Danube bridges in Serbia, closing the river to shipping for some years. With all of them now rebuilt, normal commerce has been resumed, including river cruises all the way to the Black Sea.

Meanwhile, the two-stage enlargement of the European Union to 27 nations has extended its reach along the whole course of the Danube: Hungary and Slovakia joined in 2004, Romania and Bulgaria in 2007.

The Marienberg citadel watches over the River Main at Würzburg.

istockphoto.com/Khirman

ON THE SCENE

A Danube cruise sets its own agenda. Over its entire length, the great river flows through, or past, ten Central and East-European countries. Fields, forests and picturesque villages slip by at a gentle pace. The ship ties up at a succession of charming little towns and great cities, usually close to the historic centres so you can stroll ashore to take in the principal sights.

Würzburg to Passau

Before embarking on the Danube itself, many cruises begin on the River Main, linked to it by canal. Some start at Würzburg, a proud episcopal city straddling the River Main.

Würzburg

The illustrious bishopric lies in the heart of Franconia's wine country. Vineyards spread up the slopes around the Marienberg citadel overlooking the town from across the Main river. This Renaissance fortress houses the Mainfränkisches Museum of regional art and folklore, including ancient wine-presses. But the most cherished works are the Gothic sculptures of Tilman Riemenschneider, who made Würzburg his home from 1483 to 1531.

Residenz

In the episcopal princes' Residenz designed by Balthasar Neumann and Lukas von Hildebrandt (1744), the city possesses one of the finest baroque palaces in Germany. Giambattista Tiepolo painted the Europa fresco over the grand ceremonial staircase, as well as those in the oval Kaisersaal (Imperial Hall) depicting Würzburg's medieval history. Neumann's triumph is the Hofkirche, the court church flooded with light and colour (undergoing restoration in 2012). Tiepolo contributed an *Assumption* and the *Angels' Fall from Heaven* for two side altars. Candlelit winetastings are held in the court cellars.

Neumünster

Another fine baroque church is the Neumünster, its noble façade attributed to Johann Dientzenhofer. Inside, a Riemenschneider Madonna in stone stands in the southeast niche of the rotunda. The church is the burial shrine of St Kilian, the Irish missionary martyred in Würzburg in 689. The neighbouring cathedral (rebuilt since destruction in 1945 and being renovated in 2012) is dedicated to the monk. On the south side of the transept, several Riemenschneider sculptures are placed in a modern stone setting.

Ochsenfurt

Another 20 km (12 miles) upstream you reach Ochsenfurt, whose town walls date from the 14th century. The timber-framed houses on Hauptstrasse with wrought-iron signs are particularly attractive. Here you will find the late-Gothic Rathaus (town hall), one of the finest in Franconia, whose musical clock is the town's emblem. The Andreaskirche (13th–15th centuries) has a richly decorated interior with a sculpture by Riemenschneider. Frankish traditions are upheld in many folklore festivals. Richard I of England was detained here in 1193, one of several places he was held, while returning to England from the Third Crusade.

Kitzingen

The former importance of Kitzingen, one of the oldest towns on the Main (8th century), is apparent from its Renaissance town hall and several churches dating from the 15th to 18th centuries. Parts of the town walls still remain.

Volkach

The attractive little wine-growing town of Volkach, on a loop of the Main, is worth a visit for its fine Renaissance town hall and the baroque Schelfenhaus, but especially for the pilgrim church of St Maria im Weingarten (St Mary-in-the-Vineyard) to the northwest of the town, which houses Riemenschneider's Rosenkranzmadonna (Madonna of the Rosary).

Schweinfurt

Schweinfurt is the biggest industrial centre of Lower Franconia. The city has been destroyed several times over the centuries, most recently in World War II. Nevertheless, some buildings remain to attest to its historic importance as a free imperial city, among them the late-Romanesque Johanniskirche (altered several times), the town hall (16th century), the former Gymnasium (grammar school), now the town museum, and the Zeughaus (armoury).

Hassfurt

The delightful Franconian town of Hassfurt lies 28 km (17 miles)

Main-Danube Canal. In 1992 the dreams of Charlemagne and Ludwig I of Bavaria were realised when the Main–Danube Canal between Bamberg and Kelheim was completed, opening to seagoing ships a 3,500-km (2,170-mile) waterway linking the North Sea with the Black Sea. Work on the canal began in the Middle Ages. The Ludwigskanal, with 100 locks along its 177 km (110-mile), was inaugurated with great ceremony in 1846, but competition from the railways proved disastrous. Further work was undertaken in 1922, the stretch from Bamberg to Nuremberg became navigable in 1972, and in 1992 the final stretch to Kelheim was inaugurated. The resulting waterway is an engineering marvel, with 16 locks in a total length of 171 km (106 miles).

istockphoto.com/Busto

further on. Its late-Gothic Ritterkapelle (Knights' Chapel) is embellished by a heraldic frieze with 241 coats of arms, together with interesting tombs. The Gothic Pfarrkirche (parish church) contains several works of art, including a wooden sculpture of John the Baptist by Riemenschneider.

Bamberg

Only 30 km (19 miles) to go until you reach the episcopal city of Bamberg. The old town is graced with works by Riemenschneider and the architect family Dientzenhofer. At the end of August, the old town is the site of an exuberant fair. Along with hearty Franconian dishes you can enjoy a glass of Bamberg's speciality: smoked beer (Rauchbier)!

Take a good look at the **cathedral**, where the transition from Romanesque to Gothic can be clearly traced. It houses the tomb of Emperor Heinrich II and his wife, a work by Riemenschneider, as well as the Bamberger Reiter, a remarkable Gothic equestrian statue in stone.

On Karolinenplatz stand the late-Gothic **Alte Hofhaltung** (the former episcopal palace, now housing the historical museum) and the early baroque **Neue Hofhaltung** (also called the Neue Residenz). The latter, designed by J.L. Dientzenhofer, has on the first floor a gallery of paintings by

istockphoto.com/Hollaender

istockphoto.com/Domes

Huber/Schmid

German masters, and on the second you can admire grand chambers with antique furniture and tapestries. There's a fine view of the old town and the Benedictine abbey of St Michael from the rose garden.

On an island in the River Regnitz, which once separated the castle district from the bourgeois quarter, stands the **Altes Rathaus** (Old Town Hall), decorated with 18th-century frescoes.

The picturesque fishing quarter of **Klein Venedig**, "Little Venice", lies on the right-hand bank of the river.

Bayreuth

Make a side-trip to Bayreuth, known for its annual festival of Richard Wagner's operas. The composer's home, **Villa Wahnfried**, is now a museum (closed till 2014) containing stage sets, costumes and musical memorabilia. Wagner is buried in the garden with his wife Cosima, daughter of Liszt. The Markgräfiches Opernhaus, by two theatre designers from Bologna in the 18th century, is a charming baroque creation, with three galleries festooned in stucco trimmings.

Wagner's operas find an elegant venue in Bayreuth. | Nuremberg's medieval buildings have been restored. | Traditional costumes in Ochsenfurt.

Nuremberg

A fine-looking town, Nuremberg (in German Nürnberg) can once more look with pride on its distinguished history. A centre of medieval culture and veritable heart of Renaissance art north of the Alps, it has also always been at the forefront of German industry and commerce. Today, with a population of 504,000, it dominates the northern Bavarian region of Franconia. Largely destroyed in World War II, it has been lovingly restored, and its churches, museums and culinary delicacies are incentives to spend time here.

Old Town

Near the castle, opposite the Tiergärtner Gate, the **Albrecht Dürer House** was bought by the painter in 1509. He lived there until his death in 1528. This characteristic late-Gothic patrician residence, gabled and half-timbered, has been restored as a museum of the artist's life and work.

Over at Burgstrasse 15, the **Stadtmuseum Fembohaus** (1596) is a magnificent example of Renaissance architecture and craftmanship. Inside, its fine wooden panelling, stucco work and painted ceilings make an appropriate setting for a museum of 16th–19th century domestic life.

Of the city's many ornamental fountains, look out on Rathausgasse for the 16th-century **Gänsemännchen-Brunnen**, depicting a jolly fellow in bronze carrying two geese. His good humour contrasts with the monumental pomp of the Schöner Brunnen on Hauptmarkt, where princes and prophets celebrate the old imperial glories. The marketplace is the setting of the December Nürnberger **Christkindlesmarkt**, a feast of lights, music and the good things of Christmas.

Restored to its former majesty on the market square is the **Frauenkirche**, the stepped-gable 14th-century church destroyed in 1945. Every day at noon, on the huge 16th-century clock at the top of the gabled porch, seven prince-electors come out to honour their emperor, Karl IV. Inside, the outstanding work is the 1445 Tucher Altar in the chancel, depicting in its central triptych, by an unknown artist, the Crucifixion, flanked by the Annunciation and Resurrection.

Museums

On the Kornmarkt, the **Germanisches Nationalmuseum** is housed in a Carthusian monastery. Pride of place goes to Albrecht Dürer's paintings, among them his *Lamentation of Christ*.

At Karlstrasse 13, the **Spielzeugmusem** (Toy Museum) presents a wonderful array of toys and a puppet theatre.

The German Railways' **DB Museum**, at Lessingstrasse 6, dis-

Germany's oldest stone bridge crosses the Danube at Regensburg and dates back to the 12th century.

hemis.fr/Frumm

plays a replica of Nuremberg's original Adler steam engine of 1835, along with other vehicles of historic interest.

In the Justizpalast, **Courtroom 600, Memorial Nuremberg Trials**, opened end 2010.

Berching
The small Bavarian town greets the visitor with a skyline straight out of the Middle Ages: the town ramparts (constructed around 1450), with 13 towers and four gates, are intact, and you can walk along parts of the walls.

Riedenburg
The health resort of Riedenburg became a market town in the 13th century, protected by three castles. The **Altmühl Valley** is popular with nature lovers, hikers, canoeists and cyclists alike. The Jagdfalkenhof (Falconry Lodge) at **Schloss Rosenburg** (built 1112) gives demonstrations with large birds of prey, and has an interesting Crystal Museum.

Kelheim
Here the Main–Danube Canal ends and the Altmühl flows into the Danube, which has made its way from its sources in the Black Forest in southwest Germany. The remains of the medieval walls and gates of Kelheim, founded around 1200, can still be seen. Note the Gothic parish church and the elegant façades of the baroque town houses. To the west of Kelheim, the 45-m (147-ft) Befreiungshalle (Liberation Hall), built by Ludwig I of Bavaria to commemorate the wars of liberation fought against Napoleon, crowns the Michelsberg.

Weltenburg
The Benedictine monastery of Weltenburg stands in a setting full of natural drama, where the Danube cuts a narrow gorge through the hills of the Franconian Alb. This is where the Christianization of Bavaria is supposed to have begun in the 7th century. The monastery church, a late-baroque jewel, was built in 1716–18 by the Asam brothers, who were active in south Germany but also further afield in Bohemia and Silesia. Earthly pleasures are catered for by the beer from the monastery-run brewery.

Regensburg
Like Bamberg, Regensburg survived the war almost unscathed, preserving its historical splendour. The city hails back to Roman times, when the mighty Porta Praetoria was built (see vestiges in the north wing of the Bischofshof). The diocese was founded in the 8th century, and from this time princes and emperors held their Diets in the city. Regensburg's heyday was the

ROTHENBURG OB DER TAUBER

This town south of Würzburg is the quintessence of Germany's most romantic era. Medieval ramparts, monumental gates and lofty gabled half-timbered houses, beautifully preserved, recall Rothenburg's past glories. The town is built on heights over a river valley. Serving as a natural moat beneath its western walls, the Tauber river has its source 14 km (8 miles) south of town and joins the Main river 120 km (75 miles) to the north. Begin your walk around town at the 15th-century Ratstrinkstube, now the **Tourist Information Office,** on the north side of Marktplatz. The figures on the old clock go into action on the hour from 11 a.m. to 3 p.m. and from 8 to 10 p.m.

The imposing **Rathaus** is an apt expression of Rothenburg's civic pride during its medieval and Renaissance glory. Anyone tackling the stairs to the top of the 60-m (196-ft) belfry gets a splendid view over the town and Tauber valley. To the east, the Renaissance façade (1572–78) added a fine arcade in 1681.

A 750-year-old Dominican convent houses the **Reichsstadt-museum.** Its exhibits include the monastic kitchens, medieval and Renaissance furniture, utensils, weapons and interesting memorabilia from the old Jewish community. The Hohenstaufens' castle has long gone, but the **Burgtor** city gate (1360) still stands, leading to the castle gardens with a good view of the Tauber valley.

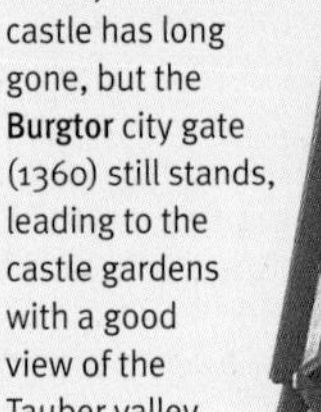

Middle Ages, and to this day the magnificence of the merchants' houses attests to their wealth and prestige. The **Steinerne Brücke** (Stone Bridge) is the oldest surviving bridge in Germany (12th-century), and connects the main part of the city with the settlement on the opposite bank.

The beautiful old city is dominated by the magnificent Gothic **Petersdom**, with its two 105-m (344-ft) spires. **St Emmeram's Basilica** dates back to the 8th century but has the Asam brothers to thank for its sumptuous baroque interior. The finest secular building in the city is probably the **Old Town Hall**.

Huber/Mehlig

Travel Pictures Ltd

Its feet almost in the water, the monastery at Weltenburg. | Inside the Walhalla.

Walhalla

A short distance downstream, a huge white marble pseudo-Grecian temple towers above the Danube: this is Walhalla, built for Ludwig I of Bavaria. Climb the 358 steps from the moorings to the hall of fame, which houses busts of eminent Germans.

Straubing

Straubing lies in the fertile Dungau, the heart of the Bavarian granary. In the picturesque Altstadt (Old Town), see the 14th-century Stadtturm with its five spires on Hauptplatz; Theresienplatz and Ludwigsplatz are surrounded by patrician houses. One of the finest churches is the Ursulinenkirche, designed by the Asam brothers. A short distance out of town, the Peterskirche is Straubing's oldest place of worship, built around 1180. One of the churchyard's three chapels is devoted to Agnes Bernauer, a barber's daughter who was drowned as a witch in the Danube.

Vilshofen

Located shortly before Passau, this town is mostly known for the **Donau in Flammen** fireworks show and its floating Christmas market.

The Danube traces a hairpin loop at Schlögen.

Huber/Gräfenhain

Passau to Vienna

The "Town of Three Rivers", Passau, stands at the confluence of the Danube, the Inn joining it from the south and the little Ilz from the north. Champions of the Inn (which gives its name to Innsbruck) note that it is broader and bluer here than the Danube, and so much more deserving of Johann Strauss's waltz. Ships moor below the proud Veste Oberhaus castle, and Austria is but a stone's throw away.

Passau

On the German side of the border, Passau (km 2227) is a solid old bishopric that has always enjoyed the good life, celebrating its religious festivities with plenty of music, beer for the men and hot chocolate for the ladies. Historically prospering from trade in wine, wheat and salt, it is an inviting city, from the bulbous onion domes and graceful arches of its baroque monuments to the rounded promontories separating the waterways.

For a fine view over the town's charming backdrop of green wooded hillsides, make your way up to **Burg Oberhaus**. The castle museum offers a good introduction to the life and times of the region's medieval inhabitants and their crafts—of old, Passau rivalled Damascus and Toledo for the delicate workmanship of its finely honed sword blades.

To the south, the core of the town stands on the ridge of land between the Danube and Inn rivers. Towering over it is the **Stephansdom**, with its three onion domes, Flamboyant Gothic chancel, rich baroque interior boasting a total of 1,000 sculpted figures, and Europe's biggest church organ, with 17,774 pipes. Recitals are held at noon from Monday to Saturday.

Through the Mühl Region

At **Lindau** (km 2222), where more Danube cruise ships dock on the German left bank, as far as the **Jochenstein** power station (lock at km 2203), the river forms the German-Austrian border. For the

Passau's pacifists. The people of Passau have always been far too fond of the good life to spoil it by wasting time fighting. When the town was besieged by the Bavarians in 1703, the bishop's three companies of soldiers declined to report for duty, explaining that they had all come down with a fever. The Bavarian forces were eventually able to complete their conquest, but not until 1741—and their general, much frustrated, complained that he had met no opposition at all!

next 323 km, it flows through Austria, at first through the wooded hill country of the Upper Austrian Mühlviertel. River travellers are charmed here by medieval villages, knights' castles, monasteries and the splendid narrow loop of the **Schlögener Schlinge** (km 2187).

The hydroelectric power stations of Aschach (km 2162) and Ottensheim-Wilhering (km 2147) oblige ships to pass once more through locks.

Linz

Standing where the Danube valley flattens into a plain, Linz (km 2135), capital of the province of Upper Austria, rises from the banks of the river at an important communications junction with Germany and the Czech Republic. The first (horsedrawn) railroad on the continent was inaugurated in Linz in 1832, running to Budweis in Bohemia, and five years later the first Danube steamships arrived, encouraging the expansion of the mining, metal, machine and textile industries. Post-war, the city concentrated on heavy industry and chemicals. In the 1990s a congress and trade fair centre was built, as well as the Ars Electronica Center. The huge Voestalpine steel plant is located across the Nibelung Bridge on the north bank, along with important chemical factories. The port, separated from the river by a protective harbour with special wharves, is Austria's biggest, handling 4 million tonnes of goods per year.

In the past, countless scholars, poets, musicians and architects found the town a most congenial

place to put down roots: Mozart and Beethoven stopped here long enough to write the Linz Symphony and the 8th respectively. Linz was designated a European Capital of Culture for 2009.

Hauptplatz

The heart of the remarkably well-preserved Old Town (Altstadt) on Linz's south bank centres around the Hauptplatz, with its stately pastel-coloured buildings from the 17th and 18th centuries and an imposing Gothic Rathaus (city hall). The magnificent baroque Jesuitenkirche cathedral (or Alter Dom) is where composer Anton Bruckner (1824–96) served as organist. In the middle of the square juts the white-marble Trinity Column (Dreifaltigkeitssäule) of thanksgiving erected in 1723. A carillon plays several times a day. A short walk away, the **Lentos Kunstmuseum** displays artworks of the 19th and 20th centuries.

Landhaus

On Klosterstrasse, a few steps away from Hauptplatz, this gracious Renaissance palace has an arcaded courtyard and flower-bedecked balconies. Its fountain depicts the planets, recalling that the German astronomer Johannes Kepler taught in this building in the 17th century, when it was a university. Today it houses the provincial government.

Schlossmuseum

The ancient castle on the Danube, one of the residences of the Emperor Friedrich III, is one of several Upper Austria museums (Landesmuseen). Its very modern south wing opened in 2009. The

SALZBURG

A golden city, Salzburg lies in an unequalled environment of mountains, hills and forest, between the left bank of the River Salzach and the Mönchsberg, topped by the Hohensalzburg fortress. Some 100 km (62 miles) south of Linz, it is a popular excursion for cruise passengers.

There is something indefinably southern about the old part of town, listed as a UNESCO World Heritage site. Many compare it with Florence or Venice. Baroque architecture lends a dreamy, poetic charm. Narrow streets lead into spacious squares, elegant settings for Gothic churches and monasteries and ornately sculpted fountains. Mansions and Renaissance palaces reign over beautiful parks and gardens.

Today Mozart haunts Salzburg. Recitals are held in the most splendid ceremonial rooms of the palaces and castles; his homes are preserved as museums. There's the Mozarteum music academy, the annual festival, and even chocolates, Mozartkugeln. The 250th anniversary of his birth in 2006 was marked by a host of events and celebrations.

A good place to start exploring is the heart of the Old Town. In the centre of **Residenzplatz** stands a large baroque fountain (1658– 61) surrounded by rearing horses. At 7 and 11 a.m., and 6 p.m., familiar melodies by Mozart ring out on the 35 bells of the 17th-century Glockenspiel, on the east side of the square. The west side is taken up by the Residenz, a palace of the archbishops founded in 1120 (the present buildings date from the 17th and 18th centuries). The south side of Residenzplatz is dominated by the huge **Dom** (Cathedral). It was built in Italian Renaissance style, with baroque overtones, between 1614 and 1655. In the first side chapel to the left of the entrance, is the Romanesque font, supported by four bronze lions, where baby Mozart was christened in 1756.

The baroque **Rupertinum**, a 17th-century palace built by Paris Lodron, houses part of the Museum der Moderne (MdM) as well as collections of drawings and photographs.

Backing into the base of the Mönchsberg, the long building of the **Festspielhaus** (Festival Hall) has been converted from the former court stables. It includes several theatres, the Haus für Mozart and other concert halls, and a riding school with three rows of seats carved out of the hillside. The 130 horses that were quartered in these palatial lodgings had the exclusive rights to the waters of the **Pferdeschwemme** on nearby Sigmundsplatz. A grandiose Renaissance structure of 1695, this splendid horse trough is ornamented with frescoes of prancing steeds, dominated by a vigorous sculpted group by Michael Bernhard Mandl depicting a man breaking in a horse.

Getreidegasse is the great shopping street of Salzburg's old town. A veritable forest of wrought-iron guild signs adorns its Renaissance and baroque façades. The houses are narrow but four or five storeys high and delving deep on each side, around alleyways and hidden courtyards (at, for example, Nos. 23, 25, 34 and 38). Number 9 is **Mozart's birthplace**—now an enchanting museum. Exhibits include manuscripts of minuets Mozart wrote when he was five, his counterpoint notebook, paintings of papa Leopold and sister Nannerl. A clavichord bears a note written by wife Constanze: "On this piano my dear departed husband Mozart composed *The Magic Flute*".

Getreidegasse opens onto Rathausplatz; continue past the Town Hall to the **Alter Markt** on your right. At No. 6, don't miss the pharmacy (Hofapotheke) that has kept its old rococo décor.

At No. 8, Makartplatz, Mozart's Residence, the **Tanzmeisterhaus**, was the family home from 1773 to 1780. It has been converted into a Mozart museum displaying his personal fortepiano.

Trinity Church, with a concave façade, is another of Fischer van Erlach's baroque masterpieces (1694–1702). The large building on the west side of the square is the State Theatre: behind it is the Marionettentheater where puppets perform *The Magic Flute*. The Mozarteum next door is the Academy of Music.

Corbis/Bianchetti

SALZKAMMERGUT

A popular round-trip east of Salzburg takes you to the lakes and spas of the Salzkammergut. On the shore of a crescent-shaped lake beneath the steep slopes of the Drachenwand and Schafberg mountains, the town of **Mondsee** grew up around a 15th-century Benedictine abbey. Some of its buildings serve as a museum recounting the life of the neolithic inhabitants of the lake region. At the southern tip of the Mondsee, a succession of tunnels and narrow roads overhung by rocks form a pass between Scharfling and St Gilgen, on **Wolfgangsee**. Mozart's mother was born in **St Gilgen**, a resort prized for its water sports facilities. You can take a paddle-steamer from here to the town of **St Wolfgang**. A place of pilgrimage since the 12th century, St Wolfgang's church has a fine altarpiece by Michael Pacher, completed in 1481, depicting the coronation of the Virgin. The famous White Horse Inn *(Weisses Rössl)* set to music by Ralph Benatzky is here, on the lakefront. East of St Wolfgang, **Bad Ischl** was one of Europe's greatest cultural centres during the reign of Franz-Joseph, who spent his summers here hunting and taking the waters. In his wake came all the big names of the 19th-century art and music world: Johann Strauss, Brahms, Franz Lehar, Nestroy, Anton Bruckner, and so on. Today you can visit the emperor's villa (Kaiservilla). Empress Sissi preferred the little marble castle (Marmorschlössl) in the park, now a photography museum. South of Bad Ischl, **Hallstatt** is one of the most picturesque of Austrian villages, a cluster of white houses squeezed between the dark lake and the wooded slopes of the Dachstein. Its salt was extracted as far back as neolithic times, as you will learn in the local museum. North of Bad Ischl, the road through the **Traun valley** was one of the great European salt routes. The section between Ebensee and Traunkirchen is hewn into the rock high above the **Traunsee**, Austria's deepest lake. At its northern end, the town of **Gmunden** has an island castle linked to the shore by a wooden walkway. The scenic route back to Salzburg takes you across to **Steinbach am Attersee** then follows the east shore of the lake. Make a halt at the lookout point at **Buchberg**.

collections include Applied Arts, coins, weapons, musical instruments (with a piano played by Beethoven) and medieval artworks. The nearby Carolingian **Martinskirche** is the oldest church in Austria to retain most of its original 8th-century form.

For a good view of the city, the surrounding countryside and the Alps, cross the river to the north bank, where a steep electric railway climbs to the top of the **Pöstlingberg**.

Touristeninformation Linz

The Lentos-Kunstmuseum at Linz is housed in a modern building on the right bank.

Linz to Mauthausen

Beyond the extensive Linz harbour and river mouth of the Traun come the locks at the Abwinden-Asten power plant (km 2120).

Mauthausen (km 2112), originally established as an imperial customs station at the confluence with the Enns river, is now more bitterly remembered as the site of Austria's largest concentration camp. A chapel and a monument remember its 100,000 victims.

Just 17 km further, there are more locks at the Wallsee-Mitterkirchen power plant.

Grein

The castle of Greinburg watches over the enchanting town (km 2079), which has a lovely rococo theatre in the main square, which has remained unaltered since it was built in 1790. Werfenburg castle in Struden (km 2076) and the picturesque ruin of Freyenstein on the right bank (km 2070) are also worth a look.

Strudengau and Nibelungengau

After the quite craggy and once dangerous Strudengau stretch of river between Dornach and Persenbeug (km 2060), a baroque castle of the Habsburgs stands on the left bank near the locks of the Ybbs-Persenbeug hydroelectric station. This is the start of one of the Danube's most romantic sections. For 24 km, it flows through the Nibelung region, scene of the song saga that inspired Wagner's operas. The baroque church of **Maria Taferl** above Marbach (km 2050) is the most important pilgrimage church in Lower Austria.

Wachau

The locks of the Melk power station (km 2038) herald the beginning of the Wachau, a UNESCO

World Heritage Site since 2000. Here the Danube conjures up dreamy thoughts in the hardiest of folk as it winds its way just 30 km (19 miles) between Melk and Krems in Lower Austria (Niederösterreich), where country villages alternate with dark castle ruins on craggy cliffs. This stretch basks in an exceptionally mild climate. The best times to see it are spring and autumn.

The Wachau is easily accessible from Vienna by road—90 km (56 miles) on the motorway—or by Danube steamship. Until 1972, when a bridge was built over the Danube near Melk, the only way to cross was by ferry.

Melk

Long before Melk (km 2036) became the home of the Benedictines in 1089, its clifftop position above the river bend made it an ideal military camp from which to fend off barbarians. Melk was settled permanently as early as the 9th century, and the Babenbergs made it their royal residence and stronghold in the 10th, although it was not to receive a charter until 1898.

In the Middle Ages, the salt, wine and iron trades flourished here, their products carried by Danube shipping. In 1548 a fire reduced the town virtually to ashes, and it was rebuilt in the Renaissance style.

Stift Melk

Having crossed the forecourt, you find yourself confronted by the impressive eastern façade of the monastery. This dates from the early 18th century, when Jakob Prandtauer was commissioned to transform the forbidding strategic fortification into a splendid baroque sanctuary with gracefully tapering towers and a majestic octagonal dome. The project was completed after his death by his pupil Josef Munggenast.

The **Marmorsaal** (Marble Hall), light, bright and richly decorated with ceiling frescoes and other ornaments, was used as a dining room and guest room in former days. Pass through the balconies overlooking the Danube to the **Bibliothek**, its magnificent inlaid shelves weighed down with some 100,000 precious books and 2000 manuscripts. The room is a precious work of art in its own right.

A spiral staircase leads down into the **Stiftskirche** (Abbey Church), where you can admire the high altar, the pulpit, the beautifully carved confessionals and choir stalls, the ceiling frescoes by Johann Michael Rottmayr and the great organ.

The treasury includes the **Cross of Melk** inlaid with pearls and precious stones. It is claimed that the cross was stolen in the 12th century. It found its way back to the monastery by mysterious means

—floating against the current upstream from Vienna! It can be seen on special occasions.

Between Melk and Dürnstein

Schloss Schönbühel stands on a rock on the right bank (km 2032). The medieval **Aggstein** robber barons' castle is perched in ruin on a rugged hilltop (km 2025).

Across the river in **Willendorf** (km 2024) the famous "Venus of Willendorf" fertility statue was found (you can see her in the Naturhistorisches Museum in Vienna).

The attractive wine village of **Spitz** (km 2019) awaits with its Hinterhaus medieval castle. The parish church at Weissenkirchen, surrounded by vineyards, combines fortifications with a house of worship (km 2013).

Dürnstein

This pretty little baroque town (km 2009) nestles on the bank of the Danube and can only be explored on foot: cars must be left on the edge of town.

Kuenringerburg

Dürnstein is famous mainly for the castle above the town in which Richard I of England, the

istockphoto.com/anzeletti

Frédérique Fasser

istockphoto.com/Frank

Melk abbey and the ornate ceiling of its Marble Hall. | The banks of the Danube are popular with cyclists.

Lion-Heart, was held captive in 1192. He had offended the Babenberg Duke Leopold V during the Third Crusade, and was recognized and captured in Vienna whilst attempting to slip away up the Danube valley. According to the legend, his faithful minstrel Blondel traced him here to Dürnstein by singing the king's favourite songs outside every castle until he came to the right one and heard Richard join in the chorus, but the captive was only released after the payment of a huge ransom; it cost England 23,000 kg of silver.

In 1645, during the Thirty Years' War, Swedish troops burned Dürnstein, leaving the Kuenringerburg in ruins. The 20-minute ascent to the castle is rewarded with fine views of the river.

Stiftskirche

The Abbey Church, resplendent in blue and white, has one of the finest baroque towers in the whole of Austria. Walk through the ornate portal and the quiet courtyard to reach the interior, where the three divine virtues Faith, Hope and Charity watch over the carved pulpit. The cloister is worth a visit.

Hauptstrasse

On Hauptstrasse, bounded to the east by the Kremser Tor, you can see many pretty town houses from the 16th to 18th centuries, some of them with sgraffito decoration. On the same street, you will find the late-Gothic **Rathaus** (town hall) with its fine courtyard. Only ruins remain of the former Klarissenkloster (Convent of the Poor Clares).

Kellerschlössl

You can take part in a wine tasting in the Kellerschlössl (1715), with its huge old wine cellar and rich decoration of frescoes and reliefs.

Krems

The centre of the Wachau's wine industry, Krems (km 2002), linked to Stein by the appropriately named village of Und ("and" in German), is considered to be the most beautiful town in Lower Austria. The three towns have merged into one. If you walk along Untere Landstrasse, past the Kleines Sgraffitohaus, you will come to the **Simandlbrunnen** ("Simon's Fountain), depicting the character in question returning home from an evening's drinking to a none-too-gentle reception from his angry wife.

Cross Wegscheid to reach Hoher Markt, the town's oldest square. Here stands the resplendent Gothic **Gozzoburg**, a patrician residence built in the 13th century in Italian style by the municipal judge Gozzo. Medieval pageants are held here.

In the **Piaristenkirche**, the church in Piaristengasse, there's an extensive collection of paintings by Martin Johann Schmidt (1718–1801), a prolific artist familiarly known as Kremser Schmidt, who adorned most of the region's churches.

The **Pfarrkirche** St Veit (St Vitus parish church) is a fine 18th century baroque building decorated by eminent artists. The large ceiling frescoes and the All Souls Altar, at the back of the church and to the right, are by Kremser Schmidt.

The Dominican church and its adjacent monastic buildings today house the **museumkrems**, which traces the development of wine-production and the town's history, including a scale model. Exhibitions, conferences and concerts are held in the early Gothic interior of the medieval church.

The **Steiner Tor**, the gate at the end of Obere Landstrasse, was part of the medieval city wall. Its round Gothic towers date from the 15th century. But for many, the most enjoyable monuments in Krems are the Renaissance houses on **Obere Landstrasse**, where they serve the new Heuriger wine in tree-shaded courtyards.

Stein

In Stein, several fine buildings face Steiner Landstrasse. The **Minoritenkirche** or Minorites' Church was built during the transition from Romanesque to Gothic, and this stylistic blend gives the building its particular character. The **Pfarrhof** (presbytery), with its fine rococo stucco work, is also worth a visit. The mighty seven-storey tower of the **Frauenbergkirche** rises above the town.

Stift Göttweig

Visible from far away, Stift Göttweig looks almost unreal sitting on its hill 425 m high a few kilometres south of the Danube. This important Benedictine monastery was founded in the 11th century and rebuilt in baroque style in the 18th century.

Tulln Basin

Ships pass through locks at the hydroelectric works of Altenwörth (km 1980) and Greifenstein (km 1949). Following a popular referendum in 1979, the nuclear power station at Zwentendorf (km 1977) was not linked up to the national power grid. The town of Tulln (km 1963) was once the Roman cavalry post of Compagna, later an important medieval trade centre.

Klosterneuburg

The Augustine abbey at Klosterneuburg (km 1939) was founded in 1114 and rebuilt by Emperor Karl VI in the 18th century to emulate the Escorial in Madrid, home of his Spanish Habsburg ancestors. His dream of a vast baroque palace-cum-church with nine domes, each graced with a Habsburg crown, had to stop short at one big dome, with the imperial crown, and one little one, with the crown of the Austrian archduke. The major attraction of the interior is the Leopold Chapel's superb 12th-century Verdun Altar with its 45 Biblical scenes painted in enamel panels. As in Krems, the other attraction is outside, in the wine gardens set amid the vineyards at the edge of the Wienerwald (Vienna Woods).

Danube Canal and UNO-City

At km 1934, the narrow Danube Canal forks off towards the Vienna city centre (Innenstadt), but heavy river traffic stays on the main river. The city's striking modern landmarks south of the Vienna Woods—the round **Millennium Tower** (km 1932) on the right bank and the **UNO-City** complex (km 1929) beyond the artificial Danube Island on the left bank—rise up until you reach the landing stages near the Reichsbrücke (km 1928).

Vienna

The population of Vienna (km 1929), Austria's capital, reflects the cosmopolitan mix of peoples once ruled by the Habsburg Empire: Hungarians, Germans, Czechs, Slovaks, Poles, Spaniards, Flemings and Italians. They have all made a contribution to the city's architecture, music and painting, but also to the cuisine of its restaurants and cafés.

Stephansdom

With its Romanesque western façade, Gothic tower and baroque altars, the cathedral is a marvellous example of the Viennese genius for harmonious compromise, melding the austerity, dignity and exuberance of those great architectural styles.

From the north tower you have a fine view of the city, and of the huge Pummerin bell cast from melted-down Turkish cannons after the 1683 siege was repelled. The present bell is a recast ver-

Renata Holzbachová

Wien Tourismus/MAXUM

Österreich Werbung

sion of the original destroyed during World War II.

Mozarthaus Vienna

At Domgasse No. 5, from 1784 to 1787, lived Wolfgang Amadeus Mozart. The modest building (sometimes called Figarohaus) was renovated to re-open on January 27, 2006 for the 250th anniversary of Mozart's birth. He wrote 11 of his piano concertos here, as well as the *Marriage of Figaro* and many other pieces.

Kärntner Strasse, Ring

From Stephansdom, the Kärntner Strasse takes you southwards through a pedestrian zone. It is the city's main north-south thoroughfare, where many of Vienna's smartest shops can be found. It leads past the world-famous Staatsoper to the Ring. This boulevard encircling the Innere Stadt was mapped out in the 1860s along the ramparts. Along it are handsome buildings such as the neo-Gothic **Votivkirche**, the **University** and **Rathaus** (Town Hall). On the Innere Stadt side is the **Burgtheater**, a high temple of the German stage. Beyond it is the lovely **Volksgarten**.

Schloss Schönbrunn put into in perspective. | Social life in winter is ruled by glamorous balls. | Distinguished members of the Spanish Riding School.

Sissi: myth and reality. Empress Elisabeth (1837–98) was an intelligent and cultivated woman who worried little about court etiquette and much about the destiny of the Hungarian people. After her marriage to her cousin Franz Joseph at the age of 16, she had to exchange a hitherto fairly free life in Bavaria for the strict supervision of her mother-in-law, Sophie. The empress fell ill, probably with a venereal disease acquired from her husband, and took refuge in the milder climate of Madeira—the first of a long series of journeys abroad. In June 1867, the imperial couple were crowned King and Queen of Hungary: the dual monarchy was born. Even this, however, did not keep Sissi in the palace. After she had given her husband four children, she decided at 40 to distance herself still further from court and pursue her passion for poetry and travel. The empress suffered a terrible blow in 1889 when her son, Rudolf, apparently committed suicide on the royal estate of Mayerling, along with his mistress, Baroness Maria Vetsera. Nine years later, when out walking on the Quai du Mont-Blanc in Geneva, Elisabeth was stabbed to death by the Italian anarchist Luigi Lucheni.

istockphoto.com/HultonArchive

From the Staatsoper, walk northwards to Albertinaplatz and on to the Hofburg.

The Hofburg

The most imposing of the imperial palaces is the Hofburg, home of Austria's rulers since the 13th century. Take the guided tour of the **Kaiserappartements**, entrance on Michaelerplatz. Some rooms of the Imperial Apartments now comprise the **Sissi Museum**.

The **Burgkapelle** (Castle Chapel), tucked away in the northern corner of the Schweizerhof, was built in 1449. The Vienna Boys' Choir (Wiener Sängerknaben) sings Mass here every Sunday morning, except in July and August.

In the **Spanische Reitschule** (Spanish Riding School), white Lippizaner horses are trained to walk and dance with a delicacy that many ballet-dancers might envy.

Schönbrunn

Schönbrunn, a UNESCO World Heritage site, is the smiling, serene expression of the personality of one woman—Maria Theresa, Archduchess of Austria, Queen of Bohemia and Hungary (Theresien in German).

Österreich Werbung

The Vienna Philharmonic Orchestra's New Year concert is always a resounding success.

Visit the gardens first. The park, laid out in the classical French manner, is dominated by the **Gloriette**, a neoclassical colonnade perched on the crest of a hill. In the palace itself, a guided grand tour (audioguides also available) will give you a glimpse of the sumptuous comfort in which Maria Theresa and her successors handled the affairs of state. A short tour takes in only the appartments of Franz-Josef and Sissi in the right wing.

Museums

Vienna's National Gallery, the **Kunsthistorisches Museum**, is outstanding. The **Naturhistorische Museum**, opposite, has zoological, anthropological and paleontological displays, and a beautiful collection of gemstones. Nearby, the modern **MuseumsQuartier** is one of the 10 biggest cultural complexes in the world, with museums, theatres and exhibition halls. The nearby Albertina displays a rich collection of works by Da Vinci, Dürer, Raphael, Rubens, Rembrandt, Klimt and Schiele.

Austrian art is displayed in three different galleries of the **Schloss Belvedere**: medieval art, the baroque museum, and the gallery of 19th and 20th century art, with works by Klimt, Schiele, Kokoschka, Munch and others.

There are museums devoted to Schubert, Haydn, Beethoven and Sigmund Freud. Vienna-born painter and architect Hundertwasser designed the **Kunst Haus Wien – Museum Hundertwasser**, on Untere Weissgerberstr. 13 in the 3rd district, using recycled material and ceramics. The museum displays a collection of the artist's works. The **Hundertwasserhaus** on Löwengasse is a shining example of non-conformism and respect for the environment.

Gumpoldskirchen

South of Vienna lies Gumpoldskirchen, one of the region's most charming wine-growing villages. Be sure to visit the 16th-century Rathaus, the Gothic church and local inns offering the new wine, "Heuriger".

Heiligenkreuz

The Cistercian abbey of Heiligenkreuz southwest of Vienna was founded in the 12th century. The Plague Column (Pestsäule) in the courtyard and the skilfully carved choir stalls are by the baroque artist Giuliani. The cloister, with its 300 red marble pillars, exudes peace and harmony. Today there is a community of around 80 monks.

Mayerling

Nearby Mayerling achieved its claim to fame through a tragic event: the 30-year-old Crown Prince Rudolf and 17-year-old

Gustav Klimt. Klimt (1862–1918) was a pioneer of modern painting in Vienna. In 1897 he became first president of the Secession group, which gathered several young artists in search of new means of expression. Having assimilated the innovative ideas and spirit of the Impressionists, Symbolists and Pre-Raphaelites, as well as the precepts of Art Nouveau, he developed a powerful personal style, at once opulent and disquieting. Among his major works, one version of *The Kiss* is displayed at the Belvedere, while his 34-m-long Beethoven frieze can be seen in the basement of the Secession pavilion.

Österreichische Galerie Belvedere Wien

Hungarian countess Maria Vetsera were found dead together in the hunting lodge—their relationship had been condemned as scandalous, and Rudolf had been refused a divorce. Emperor Franz Josef had a convent built on the spot where the couple died, and Maria Vetsera was buried in the cemetery of Heiligenkreuz, while Rudolf was laid to rest in the family tomb in Vienna.

Wien-Freudenau

Just before confluence of the Danube Canal, the Danube vessels pass the Wien-Freudenau Locks at km 1921—at the most recent and last of the nine Austrian hydroelectric stations on the Danube, opened in 1997. A much greater energy-creation project was planned further downstream in the 1980s. This would have flooded the riverbanks and destroyed the woodlands with their abundant wildlife and flora. In 1984 thousands of nature-lovers protested and succeeded since 1996 in protecting as the **Donau-Auen National Park** the last 40 km of the natural incline of the Danube as far as the mouth of the River Morava.

Petronell-Carnuntum

Some 2,000 years ago, in the region of Petronell-Carnuntum (km 1890), the Roman fort of Carnuntum was built on a site overlooking the Danube, at the frontier of the Roman Empire near the crossroads of ancient European trade routes. It was also conveniently sited for the Romans to go to the sulphur baths of what is today **Bad Deutsch-Altenburg** (km 1887) on the Hundsheim mountainside.

Hainburg

Hainburg (km 1884) likes to call itself Haydn-Stadt because the great composer, born in nearby Rohrau, went to school here. Medieval castle ruins and town gates recall Hainburg's former significance at the crossroads of trade routes.

The narrow passage at the Danube is known as Hainburg Gate, and shortly after it, on the left bank, is the mouth of the Morava (km 1880), flowing from a deep valley to mark the Austro-Slovak border. For thousands of years this gateway to the Carpathian mountains was a source of constant conflict. Both rivers were guarded by the **Devín Castle** from the time of the Celts to the 17th century. The ruin on the Slovak side is one of the Danube's most picturesque. The present day border, since 2004 an interior frontier of the EU, continues 7 km from the confluence downstream on the Danube and turns off to the south.

Renata Holzbachová

Friedensreich Hundertwasser (1928–2000). Christened Friedrich Stowasser, he altered his name to Friedensreich Hundertwasser ("Rich in Peace Hundredwater") in 1949, after three months at Vienna's Academy of Fine Arts—his only formal artistic training. Taking his inspiration from nature, the changing patterns reflected in water, the rhythms of Arabic music, he favoured the use of vibrant, saturated primary colours, and was particularly fascinated by the spiral, albeit an irregular, meandering spiral. His aversion for regular, planned architecture with strict, straight lines led him to design buildings topped with trees and houses with grass roofs, uneven floors and curving walls.

Window above the entrance to Bratislava's Old Town Hall.

Jean-Paul Minder

Bratislava to Mohács

The new Danube–Oder canal links Bratislava to trade with Poland and eastern Germany. Today its textile, chemical, oil and metal industries are offset by pleasant forests, vineyards and farmland surrounding a handsome baroque city centre.

Bratislava

With a population of 430,000, the capital of Slovakia (km 1869) commands a key position close to Austria and Hungary. Towering over it is the royal castle. The German Pressburg, Hungarian Pozsony and Slovakian Bratislava are in fact one and the same place, its successive names testifying to a rich and varied past.

Castle (Hrad)

Visible from afar, this majestic building with its four corner towers stands prominently on a hill above the Danube, gleaming white after a recent renovation. The fortress dates back to the 9th century, but alterations took place in the 17th and 18th centuries and it is now largely Renaissance in style. It was destroyed by fire in 1811 and rebuilt only after 1953. Those rooms accessible to the public hold part of the collections of the Slovakian National Museum, the Treasury and an exhibition which illustrates the history of the castle and of Slovakia and the music museum .The **Castle Gardens** offer a breathtaking view of the Old Quarter and the Danube.

Also revealing is the view across the river over **Petržalka**, a suburb of housing prefabricated with concrete slabs, erected during the Communist era for over 100,000 people. It borders on Austria, whose green hills of Hainburg are visible from here.

Old Quarter

Leave the gardens by the Gothic **Corvinus Gate**, and descend the Castle Steps to the Old Quarter. Zidovská Street boasts the finest rococo building in the city: the narrow **House of the Good Shepherd**, where you'll find an interesting clock museum.

St Martin's Cathedral

Diagonally opposite on the expressway (use the subway!), you'll see the 14th-century St Martin's Cathedral, one of the most beautiful examples of Gothic architecture in the whole of Slovakia. Between 1563 and 1830, 11 Hungarian monarchs (including Maria Theresa) and their consorts were crowned here, a fact commemorated by the golden crown topping the spire.

Main Square

From the cathedral, take the pretty route along Panská Street, lined with neat Renaissance and baroque palaces, to the Main Square. Of particular interest is the **Old Town Hall** (1325) on the eastern side. The building houses the collections of the **City Museum** (Mestské Múzeum).

Primate's Palace

Heading northeast, you will soon see the neoclassical Primate's Palace, built at the end of the 18th century. In its Mirror Hall, Napoleon and Emperor Franz I of Austria signed the Treaty of Pressburg after the crushing French victory at the Battle of Austerlitz. Part of the art collection of the City Gallery can be found here.

St Michael's Gate

Heading west, you come to the gate, part of the former fortifications of the city. The tower, now 51 m (167 ft) high, has grown since it was first built at the beginning of the 14th century. In 1758 the tower was crowned with a baroque cupola, upon which St Michael sits enthroned. From the top, you have a fine view of the old town.

Theatre and Museums

Major theatres, museums and hotels are grouped in the elegant district between the Danube (Dunaj) and the greenery of wide Hviezdoslavovo Square. At its eastern end stands the Slovak **National Theatre**, built in 1886 in neo-Renaissance style. An impressive new extension stands beside the Danube, east of the old town. The nearby **Reduta Palace**, the home of the Slovak Philharmonic Orchestra, has re-opened after renovation.

Directly on the bank of the Danube, you'll find the **Slovak National Gallery** with older and contemporary art, and the **Slovak National Museum** displaying botanical, mineralogical and other exhibits.

Danube Bridge, Nový Most

The modern cable-stayed Danube bridge is surmounted by a single 86-m (282-ft) column with a panoramic restaurant on top.

Gabčikovo Canal

The Danube flows only 23 km through Slovakia between Austria and Hungary before serving, from km 1850, as the Slovak-Hungarian frontier river. Then, however, for a stretch of 38 km, the Danube ships leave the main river just beyond Bratislava at km 1853 to navigate the Gabčikovo Canal, 500 m wide and protected on both sides by tall dikes, flowing through Slovak territory. On a spur of land at Čunovo, where canal and river part, you sail past art works—an open-air exhibition of sculptures from the modern **Danubiana Meulensteen Art Museum**, a circular building also to be seen on the river bank.

istockphoto.com/Sedmak

istockphoto.com/Muran

Huber/Micklitza

Bratislava Castle. | Oops! Watch your step! (artwork in Bratislava). | Statue of Maria Theresa on Europa Square in Komárno, Nitra, Slovakia.

istockphoto.com/Brown

istockphoto.com/Sedivec

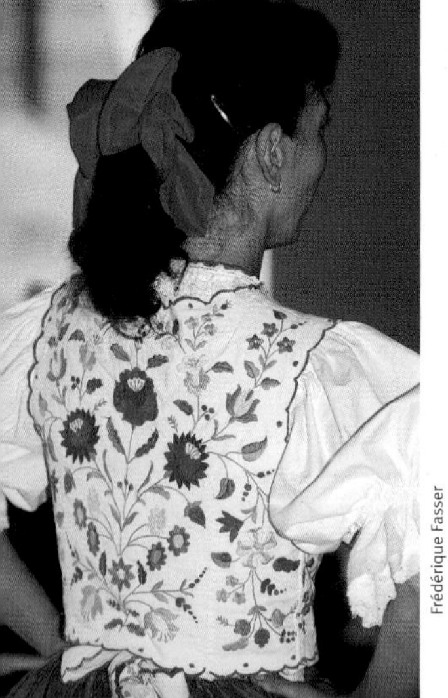

Frédérique Fasser

Two smaller arms of the Danube create giant island landscapes in the plain on either side of the main river and the canal. In the north, the Malý Dunaj (Little Danube) embraces the 80 km long Žitný ostrov (Big Debris Island) on Slovak territory, in the south on Hungarian territory, the Mosoni Duna (Mosoni Danube) flows around the 50 km long Szigetköz (Small Debris Island). The many serpentine river branches and dead arms of the river with their woody marshland shelter a significant amount of birdlife.

Some 28 km further on, the canal water is dammed at the Gabčikovo hydroelectric plant. Slovakia produces here about one tenth of its electrical energy needs. Providing a height of fall of over 20 m, the second-highest locks on the Danube were opened here in 1992. The regulation of the Danube at this point protects the hinterland from flooding and guarantees controlled water levels for ship traffic. But as more than three-quarters of the Danube water flows here through the canal, the rest of the Danube lowlands suffer occasionally from a

Basilica of Esztergom. | Time-faded splendour on the Danube bank at Esztergom. | Embroidered costumes are worn for folklore shows.

Gödöllő. Some 30 km northeast of Budapest, the town of Gödöllő is particularly well-known for its huge and handsome baroque castle. It was built from 1744 to 1748 by by Andreas Mayerhoffer for Count Antal Grassalkovich I (1694–1771). In 1867, when the emperor Franz Joseph I of Austria and his wife Elisabeth (Sissi) were crowned King and Queen of Hungary, they received it as a wedding gift.

The royal pair's regular visits gave the region a new significance. The empress came often, delighted to escape from the stiff etiquette of Vienna and to practise her favourite sport, horse riding. After her death a memorial park was built.

The castle was renovated and opened to the public in 1997. Tours include the state rooms, the park and the stables.

istockphoto.com/Lane

water shortage, threatening gradually to dry out extensive natural woodland marshes. Some 10 km downstream, the canal joins the main river again at km 1811.

Road Bridges

Three road bridges across the Danube link the Slovak left bank with the Hungarian right bank. At km 1806, the road leads 12 km south to the old bishopric of Györ, formerly Raab under the Austro-Hungarian Empire. With its break-up, the towns of **Komárno** on the Slovak side and **Komárom** on the Hungarian side (km 1768) were created in 1920. Massive fortifications on both sides of the river recall the fear of Turkish attacks in the 16th and 17th century and remain the chief sights to be seen in both towns.

The **Maria-Valeria Bridge** between Stúrovo and Esztergom (km 1719) is an expression of the new European *rapprochement*. It was first built in 1895. After its destruction by German troops in World War II (1944), a firm link between the Slovak and Hungarian towns was re-established only in 2001.

Esztergom

Some 150 km (93 miles) southeast of Bratislava, Esztergom (km 1718), was Hungary's first capital and royal seat under the Árpád kings. King Stephen was born

here around 970, and founded the cathedral in 1010. The monarchy moved out after the Mongol invasions of the 13th century, but the archbishops stayed on, taking over the royal residence. Esztergom was to pay for its ecclesiastical importance in 1543, when it was destroyed by the Turks. The restoration needed was so extensive that the Church only moved back again in 1820. And despite its clergy facing brutal persecution by the Communist authorities in the 1950s and 60s, the city has remained the centre of Hungarian Catholicism.

Basilica

The gigantic neoclassical basilica that towers over the city skyline is on the site of King Stephen's original cathedral. Begun in 1822, it took nearly 40 years to complete. The dome is based on St Peter's in Rome.

The most outstanding feature of the voluminous interior is the Bakócz Chapel, built in red marble by Florentine Renaissance craftsmen in the early 16th century. It's the only part of the old cathedral left.

To the right of the main altar, the treasury contains a magnificent collection of textiles and medieval gold relics, including the 13th-century Coronation Cross used by Hungary's kings to pledge their oaths up to the last coronation—Karl IV—in 1916. In the crypt is the tomb of Cardinal József Mindszenty. He opposed the Communist takeover after the war and was arrested and tortured. Released during the 1956 Uprising, he took refuge in the US Embassy for the next 15

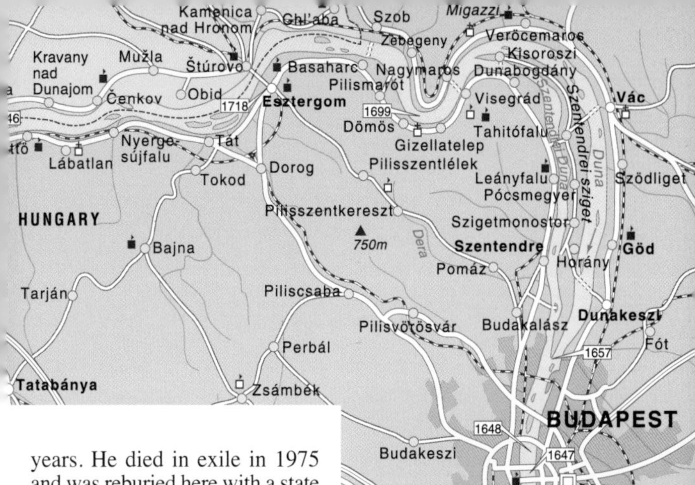

years. He died in exile in 1975 and was reburied here with a state funeral in 1991.

Complete your tour of the church by climbing up to the cupola for a superb view of both town and river.

The **Castle Museum** incorporates parts of the royal palace, including a 12th-century chapel and medieval Hall of Virtues, named after its frescoes.

Viziváros

Below the hill are the attractive baroque streets of the Viziváros, or Watertown. The **Parish Church** dates from 1738 and is in Italianate baroque style. In the old Primate's Palace, the **Christian Museum** houses what ranks as Hungary's greatest collection of religious art, with Italian prints, Renaissance paintings and the ornate 15th-century Garamszentbenedek coffin.

Beyond Esztergom

Just beyond Esztergom, the Danube forces its way between mountainsides soaring 300 and 400 m high, in places over 900 m, of the volcanic Börzsöny mountains in the north and the Visegràd range in the south, a stretch of river with glorious views over wooded hills and centuries-old little towns and castles. From km 1708, at the Danube's confluence on the left bank with the Slovak-Hungarian frontier river Ipoly, is the splendid landscape that is part of the **Duna-Ipoly National Park**. With luck, you may even spot the rare Saker falcon or Short-toed snake-eagle *(Circaetus gallicus)*, which breed in these parts.

Danube Bend

At the Danube Bend (around km 1690) the river makes a right-angle turn, from heading roughly, to almost due south. Wooded hills on either side give way here and there to pretty towns and villages dotted along the river banks. They provide an idyllic setting for the remains of King Matthias Corvinus's opulent 15th-century palace at **Visegrad** (km 1695). Much of the sprawling residence —terraced into five levels on the hillside—has been restored. The monumental Hercules Fountain is a fine example of Hungarian Renaissance; the Court of Honour has graceful arcades.

Vác

Vác (km 1680) has a pretty baroque centre, its houses still painted green, red and ochre, compensating for the textile factories and cement works on the outskirts. The 18th-century cathedral boasts remarkable frescoes by Franz Anton Maulpertsch, while the Triumphal Arch (1764) was built specially for a visit by Queen Maria Theresa.

Szentendre

Szentendre (km 1667) is a photogenic little town with a surprising number of art galleries and museums. Founded by Serbian refugees fleeing the Turks after the Battle of Kosovo in 1389, it received a second wave of Serbs three centuries later when the Turks recaptured Belgrade.

The main town square is the baroque Fő tér, with a votive cross put up by Serbian merchants in 1763 to celebrate the non-appearance of the plague. Here, too, is the green-spired Serbian Orthodox Blagoveštenska Church, built ten years earlier. The icons inside are emphatically Serbian, and evoke the troubled history of that land.

Just behind the square's east side, an alley leads to the **Margit**

Taking the Waters. You can't have everything. Hungary, occupying only one per cent of the area of Europe, lacks two significant geographical features: mountains to inspire skiers, and a seacoast. The landlocked country has to make do with the Danube and central Europe's biggest lake, Balaton. Bathing in Lake Balaton, which is rich in calcium and magnesium, is said to be good for you. The water is pleasantly warm, and your feet sink into the soft, sandy bottom, raising clouds of sand. It's certainly good for the fish: some of the pike-perch grow to 10 kg.

Any Hungarians not swimming in the Danube or Balaton are probably immersed in thermal baths. There are about 500 hot springs around the country, much appreciated since the time of the ancient Romans. Soaking in the spa waters—or drinking them—is supposed to cure just about any ailment you can imagine.

VISA/Louvet

Kovács Museum, Vastagh György 1, newly renovated and expanded. Kovács, who died in 1977, created stylized, elongated sculptures, and her work—part reinvention of religious iconic art, part folksy kitsch—is both striking and entertaining.

Skanzen

An open-air museum, 3 km northwest of Szentendre, comprises a collection of typical Hungarian houses and a wooden church of the 18th century.

Szentendre Island

Beyond Visegrád, the Danube forms the 31-km long Szentendre Island, a popular excursion-spot that continues as far as Budapest. Big ships sail along its east side. There on the left bank, they pass by Budapest's first suburbs.

Göd

The church at Göd (km 1663) is a fine example of the so-called organic architecture of its best-known Hungarian exponent, Imre Makovecs.

Budapest

The Hungarian capital Budapest (km 1648), with over 1.6 million inhabitants, conjures up a string of flattering adjectives: dramatic, enchanting, glamorous, magical. It's difficult to decide from which angle the "Paris of the East" is

Huber/Schmid

When you go shopping in Budapest's Váci utca, don't forget to look up at the splendid architecture.

most breathtaking: looking over the majestic river towards the monumental flat expanses of Pest from the heights of Buda, or rather in the direction of the hills and towers of Buda from Pest down below.

The Castle District

This fascinating zone of cobbled streets, hidden gardens and medieval courtyards hovers over the rest of Budapest on a long, narrow plateau. Towering gracefully above the old town is the neo-Gothic spire of the **Matthias Church**, founded in the 13th century by King Béla IV. The building itself is essentially 19th-century neo-Gothic, attached to what the Turks left of the original edifice in 1686. The Loreto Chapel contains the revered statue of the Virgin once buried by the Turks in the chapel walls. It is said to have reappeared miraculously during the siege of 1686.

Nearby rises an undulating white rampart with gargoyles and cloisters: the **Fishermen's Bastion**. Built on the site of a medieval fish market, it recalls the fact that in the 18th century local fishermen were responsible for defending the fortifications. The present Disneyesque structure dates from early in the 20th century. The arches frame the river artistically, as if they had been designed especially for photographers.

The Royal Palace

After a long and turbulent history, including complete destruction at the end of World War II, the palace begun in the 13th century by Béla IV has been restored to its former splendour and offers a fine view over Pest and the Danube from its walls. The building houses two excellent museums. In the baroque south wing, the **Budapest History Museum** tracks the city's evolution since the Bronze Age. Downstairs in the excavated part of the medieval castle you can see the Gothic Royal Chapel of Matthias I and the Knights' Hall. On the ground floor is a roomful of striking Gothic statues unearthed in 1974. The upper levels house collections covering prehistoric times to the arrival of the Avars. The **Hungarian National Gallery** displays an impressive modern exhibition of Hungarian art from the Middle Ages to the present day. You enter from the terrace overlooking the Danube. Among the most remarkable works, look for the splendid Late Gothic altars, so delicately carved they look like lace.

Danube Views

Gellért Hill takes its name from an Italian missionary (Gerard) who converted the Hungarians but was eventually thrown from the hill in a barrel spiked with nails, in 1046, by militant heathens. His statue stands on the north side of the hill, overlooking the Elizabeth Bridge. At the top of the hill, the severe-looking **Citadel** was built by the Austrians after the 1848 revolution. It served in World War II as the last stronghold of the German occupying army. Their bunker has been converted into the **Panoptikum** wax museum, illustrating the occupation of Budapest in 1944–45. A conspicuous modern addition to the hilltop is the **Liberation Monument**, visible from many parts of the city.

Down below, riverside Buda is known as Watertown because of its thermal baths. **Rudas Gyógyfürdő**, one of the most colourful, has been in business since 1556.

At the Buda side of the 1849 Chain Bridge, a **funicular** reaches Castle Hill just north of the Royal Palace gates. It provides one of the most scenic rides in Budapest, and has been in operation since 1870, when it was driven by steam. It was modernized and electrified in 1986.

A short walk north of the Chain Bridge in Batthyány tér, the twin-towered **St Anne's Church** is one of the most striking baroque structures in the city. Designed by a Jesuit, Ignatius Pretelli, in Italian style in the mid-18th century, the interior is a dazzling drama of huge statues and black marble columns.

The 16th-century Turkish **Király Gyógyfürdő**, with their octagonal pool, are sheltered beneath a stone dome.

Left Bank

To the northwest along the embankment, the neo-Gothic **Houses of Parliament**, looking much like their British counterpart, were built between 1896 and 1902 to symbolize the autonomy of Hungary within the greater grandeur of the Austro-Hungarian Empire. You can take a guided tour and see, among other splendours, the royal sceptre, crown and orb.

Modern luxury hotels dot the river bank as far as the Elizabeth Bridge, which sends traffic hurtling into the centre of historic Pest. The nine Danube bridges in Budapest are completed by Liberty and Petőfi bridges. South of this last stands the modern **Palace of Arts,** opened in 2005 and venue of high-class concerts, as well as the **Ludwig Museum** displaying contemporary art with works by Picasso, Baselitz, Lichtenstein alongside Hungarian artists like Endre Tót, Molnár and Erdély.

Pest

The oldest surviving structure in Pest, nestled against the flyover leading to Elizabeth Bridge, is the **Inner City Parish Church**. Founded in the 12th century, it served the Turks as a mosque.

The cobbled centrepiece of an expansive pedestrian zone, **Váci utca** is packed with shops selling wine and food, art and antiques, cosmetics, fashion and jewellery. Street vendors hawk all manner of goods. There are several cafés and restaurants where you can sit back and contemplate the street's eclectic architectural mix.

Vestiges of the city's medieval walls have been attractively incorporated into more recent buildings, notably in the streets that form part of the **Kiskörút** boulevard, bending its way from the Szabadság Bridge to Deák tér, and changing names along the way. One of its most fascinating landmarks is at 1 Vámház körút, a cavernous red-brick and cast-iron **covered market**, full of local colour and exotic smells. It opened in 1897.

The Múzeum körút section is dominated by the **Hungarian National Museum**, with a magnificent neoclassical façade. The huge exhibition covers the entire drama of the nation's history from the Stone Age to the collapse of communism. The oldest collections are on the ground floor, including extraordinary jewellery of gold and precious stones.

istockphoto.com/Butterfield

Huber/Schmid

Matthias Church in Buda, with its colourful tiled roof. | A quick way up to the Royal Palace.

Vámház körút and Múzeum körút intersect at Kálvin tér, where you might wish to make a foray into Üllöi út to visit the extraordinary building housing the **Museum of Applied Arts**. The style of this brick-and-ceramic-tile palace is listed as Art Nouveau, though it might be better described as Fantasy Hungarian with strong eastern influences.

Further south, on Páva útca, the **Holocaust Museum** was inaugurated in 2004. It includes a long-abandoned synagogue that has been magnificently renovated, as well as a new building complex. The synagogue is open to the public. The museum has permanent and temporary exhibitions.

Andrássy út, 2.5 km long, was modelled in the 19th century after the Champs-Elysées. The neo-Renaissance **State Opera House** is the most admired building on the avenue, which ends with a flourish at **Heroes' Square**, with the Millenary Monument as its centrepiece, topped by a statue of the Archangel Gabriel. Facing each other across the Square are two neoclassical buildings. The larger one is the **Museum of Fine Arts**, whose comprehensive collection of paintings, including a number of French Impressionists, gives it an international importance. The smaller **Art Gallery** holds temporary exhibitions of paintings by Hungarian and foreign artists.

Among the amenities of the **City Park** is the Castle of Vajdahunyad, modelled on a Transylvanian castle. It houses the Hungarian Museum of Agriculture. Outside is a hooded figure representing the 12th-century chronicler Anonymus. You'll notice the triple dome of the **Széchenyi Baths**, one of Europe's largest spa complexes. The sight of people playing chess while soaking in the healing waters is not to be missed.

South of Budapest

On this stretch, the Danube is bordered by dense shrubbery and trees, on the right for the first 100 km south of Budapest most often a tall river bank on which villages are more frequently seen than in the flat country on the left bank.

Dunaúváros

The steel centre of Dunaújváros (km 1578), designed after World War II, was built with its large harbour on the site of the Roman military base of Intercisum. The industrial town has a garden of archaeological ruins and a museum devoted to the Roman fortifications.

Dunaföldvár

Dunaföldvár (km 1560), where a road and rail bridge spans the Danube, recalls the era of Turkish invasions with its Turkish bastion and the castle museum.

Harta

Harta (km 1546) on the left bank dates back to Swabian (German) settlers brought here by Austria's Archduchess Maria Theresa in the 18th century.

Paks

The major attractions here are the Church of the Holy Ghost designed by Imre Makovecs and the renowned fish-soup of Paks (km 1531), as well as the country's only nuclear power station south of town (km 1526).

Kalocsa

The farming town of Kalocsa (km 1516) has something for every taste—history, folklore, art, and one of Europe's most offbeat museums. Kalocsa was founded in the 11th century alongside the Danube, but the river subsequently changed its mood and its course, leaving the town 6 km from the nearest fish or boat. Happily, the newly enlarged boundaries of Kalocsa included fertile meadows, where fruit and vegetables and grain grow. The dominant crop, though, is red paprika. So it is that Kalocsa offers the **Paprika Museum**, where you can follow the saga of the Mexican hot pepper through its Hungarian naturalization. It did not become an essential ingredient of the Hungar-

The Puszta. Also known as the Great Plain (Nagy Alföld), the vast, flat prairie of the Puszta was Hungary's very own Wild West during the 19th century, when huge herds of cattle grazed here watched over by cowboys, called gulyás. It was once covered in thick forest, but was laid waste during the Turkish occupation, because of the invaders' need for timber to build fortresses, and became a virtual desert. Its renaissance as pastureland was due to the irrigation works on the River Tisza employed by Count Széchenyi in the early 19th century. But by the 20th century, the success of the irrigation scheme meant it could sustain crop development, and big landowners carried out wholesale enclosure, killing off the cattle industry and creating widespread poverty among the peasants. Under post-war communism, the estates were nationalized, and huge collective farms introduced, only to be broken up after 1989 and returned to private ownership. Today, you will find pleasant little towns—Kecskemét and Szeged in particular are worth spending time in—beyond which are attractive old whitewashed farmsteads adorned with bright-coloured strings of paprika.

istockphoto.com/Ferenc

A fleeting encounter in the Kiskunság National Park.

ian diet until the early 19th century. One of the town's most photogenic features is the display, every autumn, of bright red peppers hanging to dry from the eaves of local houses.

Main Square
Kalocsa's main square, Szabadság tér, features statues of two national heroes—King (Saint) Stephen and Franz (Ferenc in Hungarian) Liszt. The 18th-century **cathedral**, in graceful baroque style, stands on the site of a series of churches, going back to the 11th century. In the **Archbishop's Palace** across the square, the library contains over 100,000 volumes, including a Bible autographed by Martin Luther.

Károly Viski Museum
In Kalocsa there's no shortage of folklore exhibits. The peasant costumes are a delight of floral designs. Here, too, are displays of traditional farm tools, antique furniture and decorations.

Schoeffer Museum
A master of kinetic art, Nicolas Schoeffer (1912–92) donated some of his works to his home town; they are displayed in his house of birth, at Szent István Király út 76, the same street as the Viski Museum.

Museum of Folk Art
Run by the Kalocsa Folk Art Cooperative, the museum displays antique agricultural implements and rustic furnishings. Kalocsa embroidery is on show—and on sale—and they stage folklore exhibitions in which the local youngsters dance to typically vivacious Hungarian music.

Puszta
The Hungarian version of the wild west conjures visions of gallant horsemen, lonely shepherds, pastures and dunes. It's all still there in Kiskunság National Park,

35,000 protected hectares (86,000 acres) of dramatic landscape between the Danube and the Tisza. Accomplished horsemen in baggy trousers and red waistcoats show the tourists their skills in a cross between a rodeo and a circus. Apart from the handsome horses there are herds of big-horned cattle and Racka sheep with screw-shaped horns.

One of the highlights of a visit to the puszta is a stop at a *czárda*, or wayside inn, where the food is as rustic as the surroundings. The meal is washed down with hearty Hungarian wine and the wail of gypsy violins, or the spirited melodies of the czárdás.

Kiskunság National Park

In the sandy highlands between the Danube and the Tisza, the park (760 sq km) comprising nine separate areas, preserves for posterity the historical landscapes of the Puszta and important nature reserves. Most of them have been declared UNESCO Biosphere Reserves. You will come across the region's typical domestic and pasturing animals as well as rare bird species such as spoonbills, purple herons and silver herons.

Sió Valley

Just beyond a modern motorway bridge (km 1499) spanning the now slowly flowing Danube, surrounded mostly by lush marshy

woodland is the confluence with the River Sió, transformed here into a canal for its 123-km course from Lake Balaton, plied by pleasure boats and ships.

Szekszárd

Above the Sió Valley, about 15 km west of the Danube, Szekszárd is the centre of a wine-growing region. The county seat, it has a high proportion of citizens of German and Serbian descent. Their pedigree can be traced back to the 150 years of Turkish occupation, when Szekszárd was a ghost town. To renew the population in the 18th century, settlers from neighbouring countries were welcomed. Local history starts in the 11th century, when King Béla I founded a fortified Benedictine monastery on a hill. The courtyard of the present County Hall is built around the remains of an ancient chapel and the abbey church.

Baja

Along a stretch of the Danube surrounded by virgin forests as far as Baja (km 1479), you reach the southernmost Hungarian bridge on the Danube. Over this vital link between east and west Hungary carries rail traffic as well as cars and trucks (eastbound and westbound alternate), all on a single lane. Long before there was a bridge, the Turkish invaders, aware of the strategic significance, fortified the town. Today the enormous main square, Béke tér, gives an idea of the historic importance of Baja.

Duna-Drava National Park

From the lower reaches of the Sió in the north to Hungary's southern border, the park covers a surface of 500 sq km through which the Danube flows for 65 km as well as a portion of its Drava tributary. Across the sometimes narrow, sometimes several kilometres wide floodplain with often impenetrable forest, countless tributary streams, dead arms of the river and stagnant pools form a landscape constantly changing with the considerable seasonal variations in water levels. Danube travellers make their way for hours through this wild landscape of water, woods and islands along the meandering branches of the main river. White egrets and grey herons, cormorants and wild ducks throng the banks, osprey and black stork breed on the reserve.

Gemenc Forest

Nature lovers can explore this northwest area of the national park along nature trails via a narrow-gauge railway and on boat tours. Besides rare birds, they may also spot deer, stag, beaver and wild boar.

Mohács

The Danube port city of Mohács (km 1447) is forever linked with a melancholy chapter in Hungarian history. It unfolded swiftly, a few kilometres out of town, on August 29, 1526. A well-equipped army of Sultan Suleiman the Magnificent, with a four-to-one advantage in manpower, crushed the defending forces of the Hungarian King Louis (Lajos) II. The king died during the retreat. For the next century and a half Hungary endured Ottoman occupation.

The modern **Votive Church** in the centre of town is one of the local memorials to these events. Meant to give thanks for the eventual expulsion of the Turks, it might be mistaken for a mosque, but for the dome topped by a big cross.

On the actual site of the battle, a **Memorial Park** is strewn with haunting modern sculptures symbolizing the opposing forces. The ghosts of the generals, the soldiers and the horses—in imaginative wood-carvings—are forever deployed across the field of battle. The park was dedicated in 1976 on the 450th anniversary of an unforgettable defeat.

The people of Mohács celebrate the departure of the Turks at Carnival time, when they parade in the scariest giant masks. The Busó carnival also aims to expel another invader—winter.

PÉCS

On the southern slopes of the Mecsek hills, west of Mohács, 200 km south of Budapest, the university town of Pécs (population 155,000) is the largest city in Transdanubia. Chosen as European Capital of Culture in 2010, the city is being rejuvenated, and the historic core carefully restored. On the ancient trade route from the German-speaking countries to the Balkans and Middle East, Pécs unites cultures of east, west and south.

You will see traces left behind by the former inhabitants, Celts, Romans, Turks, Germans and Hungarians. In Roman times, Hadrian called the town Sopianae and made it the capital of Pannonia. Some parts of the **Roman aqueduct** can still be seen, and many fine relics of prehistoric and Roman times are displayed in the **Archaeological Museum** at Széchenyi tér 12.

The Hungarians conquered the area in the late 9th century and their king Stephen (István, 997–1038) made Pécs an ecclesiastical centre. The first **cathedral** burnt down in 1064, but it was replaced in the 11th century by the building you see today at the top of Dóm tér. Each of its four corners are topped by a tower. The crypt, with its five naves, is the oldest part of the building; the cathedral was reworked in the 19th century in the Tuscan Romanesque style, seen in the eleven arches of the south façade. In Roman times, the square was the centre of a cemetery and many early Christian burial vaults have been excavated. This **necropolis** is a UNESCO World Heritage Site and opened to the public in 2007.

King Matthias built the circular, crenellated **Barbacan**, a gate tower for the castle. It stands next to the Bishops' Palace. After the Battle of Mohács in 1526, the Ottoman army invaded Pécs. The city was occupied by the Turks from 1543. Churches were turned into mosques, Turkish baths and minarets were built, and a bazaar replaced the market. The Turks also introduced new kinds of grapes, among them *kadarka*.

After the expulsion of the Turks, Pécs became part of the Habsburg Empire. The large main mosque, built in honour of Pasha Kasim, has been transformed into the parish church. It stands at the top of Széchenyi tér. The high round dome and striped arches remain from the Muslim era, but the congregation is now

Hungarian and Catholic, and a crucifix stands over the prayer niche. A marble tablet inscribed in elegant Arabic calligraphy spells out a verse of the Koran translated into Hungarian.

On Rákóczi út, another mosque, **Pasha Hassan Yakovali** is still a place of Muslim worship and a small museum displaying Turkish armour, stirrups, rugs, pottery and utensils; it is the only mosque in Hungary whose minaret is intact.

From the early 18th century, under the Habsburgs, the city flourished. Queen Maria Theresa granted Pécs the status of a free royal town. The architecture of many grand residences and public bulding in ornate baroque style dates back to this period.

Industry continued to develop in the second half of the 19th century: iron foundries, paper-makers, sugar-refineries and coal-mining were significant, and the **Zsolnay Porcelain** works were established in 1853. Zsolnay majolica adorns many of the town house façades. The 1869 **Synagogue,** on Goldmark Károly utca, bears a plaque honouring the local victims of Auschwitz—88 per cent of the city's Jews perished in World War II.

By the early 20th century, Pécs had developed to become one of Hungary's biggest towns. Its citizens built Eclectic-style houses, a splendid National Theatre on Kossuth Lajos utca, a fine Town Hall, coffee houses, and an ornate railway station. The only Art Nouveau building in the city, the main **Post Office** on Jókai utca bears witness to this period.

David Warden

The porcelain bull's heads decorating the Zsolnay Fountain have a metallic sheen.

One of Péc's famous sons was Victor Vasarely (1906–1997); the father of Op-Art donated many of his works to the city; they are displayed in the **Vasarely Museum** on Káptalan utca. Opposite is the Decorative Arts section of the Janus Pannonius Museum, with Zsolnay ceramics.

Can you stay in Vienna long enough to try all the different kinds of cakes and coffee?

Österreich Werbung

DINING OUT

Your Danube cruise will take you on a culinary voyage of discovery. After the hearty dishes of Germany you enter the realm of Austrian breaded cutlets and dumplings, cream-drenched cakes and pastries. Things spice up in Slovakia with its homely stews, while Hungarians claim that their cuisine is one of the best in the world.

Germany

Traditional German food relies heavily on soups, stews, roasts and many varieties of sausage. The Danube flows through Bavaria, known for its beer and for its *Weisswürste*, white veal sausages flavoured with pepper and onions and served with sweet mustard. The locals like to eat them as a midday snack before starting on a proper lunch. Try also *Blaue Zipfel*, finger-sized sausages poached with onions in vinegar, and grilled *Bratwürste*. A favourite soup is *Leberknödelsuppe*, liver dumplings in beef bouillon. Main dishes include *Kalbsvögerl*, veal roll stuffed with onion, morel mushrooms, garlic and sour cream, and *Schweinebraten*, roast pork with herbs.

Succumb to desserts such as *Schmarren*, baked pancakes with apples and raisins, and *Zwetschgendatschi*, pastry with plums, cinnamon and sugar.

Germany's wines, predominantly white, are many and varied and to foreigners may seem confusingly named. But among them there is something to suit most tastes, whether as an apéritif or to go with dinner. Franconia, the region around Würzburg and Bamberg, produces fresh white wines to put in its famous bockbeutel, round-bellied bottles.

Austria

The emperors and archdukes have gone; not so the Bohemian dumplings, Hungarian goulash, Polish stuffed cabbage and Serbian *shashlik*. But there are Austrian specialities too: *Wienerschnitzel*, a large thinly sliced cutlet of veal sauteed in a coating of egg and seasoned breadcrumbs; *Backhendl*, boned deep-fried chicken prepared like *Wienerschnitzel*; *Tafelspitz*, boiled beef, a Viennese favourite; or *Knödel*, dumplings served with soups and with the meat dish, studded with pieces of liver or bacon. Other main courses you will find include roast meats (*Rostbraten*) with garlic, and in rural areas *Bauernschmaus*, which literally means "farmer's feast". With the Danube on the doorstep, fish turns up on many menus: trout, zander (pike-perch), pike and carp are prepared in various tasty ways.

Dumplings are also served as a dessert with hot apricot inside (*Marillenknödel*) or with cream cheese (*Topfenknödel*). As for pastries, the variations of cherries, strawberries, hazelnuts, walnuts, apple and chocolate in tarts, pies, cakes and strudels are endless, and they are all even better topped with whipped cream (*mit Schlag*). And you can join in the never-ending controversy over the famous chocolate cake, the Sachertorte—whether it should be split and sandwiched together with apricot jam, or just left plain. The local wines are mostly white, and people are happy to drink white wine with either meat or fish. The best known, Gumpoldskirchner, has the full body and bouquet of its southern vineyards, but Grinzinger, Sieveringer and Neustifter are equally popular. From the Danube valley, with an extra natural sparkle, come the Kremser, Dürnsteiner and Langenloiser. One way to enjoy them is to visit a *Heuriger*, where you drink young white wine and help yourself to a buffet of hot and cold snacks, usually including cheese, cold meats and salads.

A Quick Coffee. Not likely. In Vienna a coffee is to be savoured slowly, not swallowed down in a few gulps. The choice is confusingly large. Here are a few explanations:
Brauner: black with a dash of milk.
Einspänner: black with whipped cream, served in a tall glass.
Eiskaffee: black with whipped cream and vanilla ice cream.
Kapuziner: cappuccino, topped with a dollop of whipped cream and sprinkled with powdered chocolate.
Melange: frothy and milky, maybe with a blob of whipped cream.
Mocca: strong and black, most often espresso.
Türkischer: boiling hot and sweet.
To go with your *Jause* (afternoon cup of coffee) there are plenty of delicious pastries and strudels, stuffed with poppy seeds, nuts, curd cheese or apricots.

Slovakia

In Bratislava's restaurants, you might try the local specialities:

spicy beef goulash à la Bratislava or fiery shish kebabs with pork, beef and lamb (together with ham, sausage, peppers and onions). With them come side dishes of vegetables and various potato concoctions including dumplings. *Loksa* are potato pancakes, often served with roast meats. Smoked cheese is another speciality, fried with ham and served with tartare sauce.

Local wines are mostly white, from the Veltliner, Sylvaner and Riesling grape varieties, and have sonorous names such as Malokarpatské zlato ("Gold from the Little Carpathians").

Hungary

A popular appetizer is *libamájpástétom*, flaky pastry filled with goose-liver pâté. *Hortobágyi húsos palacsinta* are pancakes filled with minced meat and sour cream; *gombafejek rántva*, breadcrumb-coated fried mushrooms. Now for the goulash, which is not at all a spicy stew, but a thinnish soup. Called *gulyásleves*, it combines bits of beef, vegetables, caraway seeds and paprika for colour and zing. *Szegedi halászlé*

istockphoto.com/Izso

Österreich Werbung

istockphoto.com/CapturedNuance

Touristeninformation Linz

Heart-warming Hungarian goulash, the real thing. | Wiener Schnitzel. | Plenty of wines to choose from. | And for dessert, a big slice of trellised Linzer torte, filled with jam.

HUNGARIAN WINES

Hungary will keep the most demanding wine-lover in a state of bliss. It's a huge producer of quality wines, though few are household names abroad. The renowned Tokaji (or Tokay) as the jewel in its crown—the wine of kings and the king of wines. Made in the Tokaj region of the Northern Uplands, it uses native Furmint and Hárslevelü grapes and ranges from the pale, dry Tokaji Furmint to the rich amber Tokaji aszú dessert wine. The latter is one of the world's great sweet wines and has had its praises sung by Louis XIV, Beethoven, Schubert and Robert Browning. Its degree of sweetness is expressed in *puttonyos*, numbered from 3 to 6 (the sweetest) and indicating the quantity of baskets (*puttony*) of "noble" grapes added to each barrel of wine.

More popularly identified with Hungary is Bull's Blood from around Eger (Egri Bikavér), a red table wine whose name tells you all you need to know about its full-bodied character. It matches with Hungary's abundance of meaty dishes, as do the younger reds, Kékfrankos and Kékoportó, and the fine Villányi-Burgundi.

But most of the country's wines are white. To accompany Lake Balaton fish, you should try a Lake Balaton wine. From the vineyards around Badacsony, on the north shore, look for a range of white wines using well-known grape varieties, including Olaszrízling, a medium-bodied Riesling, Traminer and Pinot Blanc.

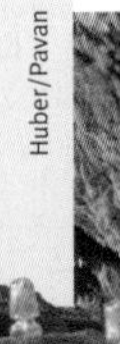

Huber/Pavan

is a freshwater fish soup. On a hot day, cold fruit soups (*hidegyümölcsleves*), made from cherries or apricots, are refreshing.

For the fish course, try *paprikás ponty*, carp with paprika sauce; *rácponty*, carp stew with sour cream; or *pisztráng tejszín mártásbán*, baked trout with cream.

Hungarians are extremely fond of large helpings of meat. *Pörkölt* or *bográcsgulyás* is the spicy stew that non-Hungarians call goulash. On menus you'll see *paprikás csirke*, chicken with sour cream and paprika. *Töltött paprika* are stuffed peppers; *bélszin Budapest módra* is a thick beef steak served with a sauce of peppers, mushrooms, peas and chopped chicken livers.

The Hungarians excel in the dessert department, so be sure to save room for a strudel *(rétes)* filled with *almás* (apple), *mákos* (poppy seeds), *meggyes* (sour cherries) or *túrós* (lemon, raisins and cottage cheese); or *Gundel palacsinta*, pancakes with a rich filling of chopped walnuts and raisins, covered in chocolate sauce and flambéed with brandy or rum.

Huber/Schmid

istockphoto.com/Coscubiela

Budapest's elegant Café Gerbeaud on Vörösmarty Square. | A colourful and appetizing selection of vegetables on Vienna's Naschmarkt.

Traditional petitpoint is not a lost art in Vienna.

Konstantin Kovačec

SHOPPING

There's no lack of opportunities for buying souvenirs of your trip, from petitpoint embroidery and chocolate Mozartkugeln, to hand-painted Hungarian porcelain.

Germany

The shops are enticing, full of quality products beautifully displayed, whether it's food, clothing or the high-tech goods for which Germany is renowned. Toys are among the most attractive buys, from perfect replica trains and cars to charming dolls in regional folk costume. Fine porcelain is another speciality, both in reproductions of 18th-century pieces and in modern designs. Look in the museum shops for superb art books and lithographs.

Austria

Not surprisingly, among the great attractions in Vienna—a city preoccupied by its history—are its antiques. Furniture and objets d'art from all over the old empire have somehow ended up here in the little shops in the Innere Stadt. Still in the realm of the past are the specialist coin- and stamp-dealers (where else could you expect to find a wide selection of mint-condition pre-1914 Bosnia-Herzegovina and other imperial issues?).

The national Augarten porcelain workshops still turn out hand-decorated rococo china-ware. Exquisite petitpoint embroidery is available in the form of handbags, cushions and other items with flower, folk and opera motifs. You will find the more elegant shops on the Kärntnerstrasse, Graben and Kohlmarkt.

If your taste runs from the exquisite to kitsch, try your luck in the Saturday morning flea market on the Naschmarkt, with plenty of food stalls, too.

Craft products include pottery and jewellery. Small watercolours or copperplate engravings of the local landscape make a charming gift. Dolls in traditional costume are a popular buy, and a good bottle of local wine or apricot schnapps will go down well.

Slovakia

For souvenirs look in the shops of the Old Quarter selling embroidery and lace, handpainted porcelain, jewellery, wood carvings and fine crystal glass. The word Starozitnosti indicates an antique shop, but not everything inside will be old; you may find attractive drawings, watercolours and prints as well as bric-a-brac and assorted junk. A characteristic Slovak craft is wire-smithing, creating decorative objects such as birds, animals or farm carts by shaping wire. Many toys are charming, especially the comical carved wooden animals.

Hungary

Hungarian woodcarving is always popular—especially striking are Hussar chess sets painted in the bright colours of the famous brigade's uniforms. In Budapest one of the best places to look for these is the first floor of the Great Market Hall. Falk Miksa utca is Budapest's main street for antique shops. Some other good buys include articles crafted from copper, brass or silver; leather goods; handmade carpets and rugs in traditional patterns; embroidered shirts, blouses and table linens. In food markets you will find sachets of ground paprika; spicy dried sausage; a garland of dried cherry peppers; packaged cake or strudel; a bottle of wine or fruit brandy. Music lovers will find a vast selection of CDs: Liszt, Kodály and Bartók, gypsy violins and folk music.

Hungarian Porcelain. Ceramics and porcelain are among the most popular products with visitors to Hungary. Two names in particular stand out. The Herend Porcelain Factory is based in the town of Herend near Lake Balaton and has been making exquisite hand-painted vases, dishes, bowls and statuettes since 1826. Herend has proved especially popular with royalty—satisfied customers include Queen Victoria, Kaiser Wilhelm I, the Shah of Iran and Prince Charles. Find out why at the main Herend shop behind Vörösmarty tér on V. József Nádor tér 11.

Zsolnay porcelain from Pécs might not be able to claim as famous a client list, but its products have been far more prominently placed. The company developed a line in brilliant weatherproof ceramic tiles in the late 19th century, and these adorn the rooftops of Matthias Church, the Central Market and the Museum of Applied Arts. Check out their modern Art Nouveau-influenced designs at V. Kígyó utca 4.

THE HARD FACTS

To help you plan your trip, here are some of the practical details you need to know about the lands along the Danube.

Climate

Most of the Danube valley has a continental climate. Winters can be harsh, with occasional snow; in January and February the temperature may drop to –15°C (–9°F). In summer it can climb to 30°C (86°F) or more, and the cities in particular can become very hot and humid, especially in July and August. It is cooler and more pleasant in the mountains or on the Black Sea coast. From April to June, September and early October are likely to be pleasantly warm. Showers are possible, even occasional thunderstorms.

Communications

Most mobile phones are compatible with at least one service provider in each country. If using the fixed line system, it is cheaper to use public telephones with a telecard rather than hotels. To make international calls, dial the access code (00 from most European countries), followed by the country code and number, usually omitting the initial 0.

The international dialling code to Austria is 43, Germany 49, Hungary 36, Slovakia 421.

Internet cafés are to be found in every town and city, and larger hotels have business centres with internet access.

Customs Controls

When crossing borders between EU and non-EU countries, or between two non-EU countries, passengers over 17 can carry, duty-free, up to 200 cigarettes or 50 cigars or 250 g of tobacco, 1 litre of spirits, 1 litre of wine (2 l for some countries), a bottle of perfume. Within the EU, you can carry much larger amounts, but only goods on which duty has been paid.

Emergencies

Most European countries have adopted the common emergency telephone number 112, which also applies to GSM mobile phones. Help from your home country's consulate is only for critical situations, lost passports or worse, not lost cash or tickets.

Essentials

Take comfortable walking shoes, a sun hat, sun-block with a high protection factor and insect repellent. It is worth taking an umbrella. You'll need lightweight cotton clothes in summer, with a sweater or wrap for the cooler evenings. People tend to dress elegantly for the theatre, concerts and the opera.

Formalities

You will need a valid passport. No special health certificates are required by European or North American citizens.

Health

There is a reciprocal health care agreement between EU countries; you must carry a European Health Card. Travellers from outside the EU should ensure that they have adequate medical insurance. Medical services are of a good standard. Many doctors and dentists speak some English. Carry supplies of any medications that you require regularly.

Money

Currency in **Germany**, **Austria** and **Slovakia** is the Euro, divided into 100 cents. Coins: 1, 2, 5, 10, 20 and 50 cents, 1 and 2 euros; banknotes: 5, 10, 20, 50, 100, 200 and 500 euros.

In **Hungary**, the *forint* (Ft. or HUF) is issued in coins from 5 to 200 Ft and banknotes from 500 to 20,000 Ft. Retain all currency exchange receipts to re-exchange *forints* when leaving the country. Do not change money on the street. Hungary is expected to adopt the Euro in 2014 at the earliest.

Opening Hours

Banks

Austria. Monday to Friday 8 or 9 a.m.–3 or 3.30 p.m., till 5 p.m. on Thursdays. Small branches may close for lunch, between 12.30 and 1.30 p.m.

Germany. Monday to Friday 9 or 10 a.m.–12.30 p.m. and 1.30–4 or 5 p.m. (longer hours on Thursdays, shorter on Wednesday or Friday).

Hungary. Monday to Friday 9 a.m. –2 p.m., Saturday 9 a.m.–noon.

Slovakia. Generally open Monday to Friday 8 a.m.–5 p.m.

Shops

Austria. Generally open Monday to Friday 9 a.m.–6 or 6.30 p.m. and Saturday 9 a.m.–5 p.m. Some have late closing (7.30 p.m.) Thursday or Friday.

Germany. Most shops open Monday to Friday 9 or 10 a.m.–7 or 8 p.m.; on Saturdays shops close earlier.

Hungary. Weekdays 10 a.m.–6 p.m. (Thursdays to 8 p.m.), Saturday 9 a.m.–1 p.m.; food shops open as early as 6 or 7 a.m.

Slovakia. Usually open Monday to Friday 9 a.m.–6 or 7 p.m. and Saturday 9 a.m. –noon or 1 p.m. Some shops also open on Sunday mornings. Smaller shops close for lunch noon to 2 p.m.

Post offices

Across the region, post offices generally open Monday to Friday 8 a.m.–6 p.m., Saturday 8 or 9 a.m.–noon or 2 p.m. Not all post offices are open on Saturdays. In Austria most close for lunch, noon to 2 p.m.

Photography and Video

Some museums allow you to take photographs but generally without using the flash; check that yours is switched off. Don't even think of taking pictures of military installations.

You will need a spare memory card for your digital camera, and don't forget your battery charger.

Public Holidays

Austria

January 1 New Year's Day
January 6 Epiphany
May 1 Labour Day
August 15 Assumption
October 26 National Day
November 1 All Saints
December 8 Immaculate Conception
December 25 Christmas
December 26 St Stephen's Day
Moveable: Easter Monday,

istockphoto.com/Niedzieski

Österreich Werbung

istockphoto.com/Karras

Ascension, Whit Monday, Corpus Christi

Germany (Bavaria)
Holidays in Germany are determined by each state; these are for Bavaria.

January 1	New Year's Day
January 6	Epiphany
May 1	Labour Day
August 15	Assumption
October 3	Day of Unity
November 1	All Saints
Dec. 25–26	Christmas

Moveable: Good Friday, Easter Monday, Ascension, Whit Monday, Corpus Christi.

Hungary

anuary 1	New Year's Day
March 15	National Day
May 1	Labour Day
August 20	National Day (St Stephen's)
October 23	Republic Day
November 1	All Saints
Dec. 25–26	Christmas

Moveable: Easter Monday, Whit Monday

Slovakia

January 1	Foundation Day
January 6	Epiphany
May 1	Labour Day
May 8	Liberation Day
July 5	St Cyril and St Methodius
August 29	Slovak National Uprising
September 1	Constitution Day
September 15	Our Lady of Sorrows
November 1	All Saints Day
November 17	Freedom and Democracy Day
Dec. 24–26	Christmas

Moveable: Good Friday, Easter Monday

Public Transport
The big cities on the Danube are served by networks of buses, trams and metro systems which are reliable and inexpensive. They mostly operate 4.30 a.m. to midnight.

Although more expensive in Germany and Austria, taxis are generally good value elsewhere along your route, and a convenient way to get around big cities such as Budapest. However, make sure the meter is working, switched on and set to zero. If there is no meter, agree the price in advance.

Safety
The cities are fairly safe by Western standards. It is nonetheless worth taking some basic precautions. When you go sightseeing, leave your valuables and important documents in your hotel or cruise ship safe. Only carry the money you will need for the day, along with a credit card.

Watch out for pickpockets in crowded areas such as markets and on public transport, and in restaurants and cafés, do not leave your bag on the floor. Beware of scams (such as money changing and phoney "distractions") aimed at foreigners, which will end up with you and your money parting company.

Sales tax (VAT)

A tax averaging 20 per cent is imposed on most goods in the EU member states, and in most other European countries. To benefit from a tax refund, your purchase in any one store must be above a certain minimum amount: look for the Tax Free for Tourists sign. The sales assistant will give you a Tax Refund Cheque (TRC) and all the necessary information on how to redeem it for cash.

When you leave the last EU country on your itinerary, take the TRC with your purchases, receipts and passport to the Customs desk to get it stamped. There may be a Tax Free booth near the Customs desk where your stamped TRC can be redeemed immediately, or you can mail the papers back to the store in the envelope they will have provided. For more information and advice see the site: www.global-blue.com.

Time

UTC/GMT +1 in winter, +2 from end March to end October for daylight saving time.

Tipping

A service charge is automatically added to restaurant bills in **Austria**, but it's customary to round the bill up by about 10 per cent. You should leave a small tip in cafés. Tips for taxi drivers are about 10 per cent.

In **Germany**, a service charge is usually included. A small extra tip is at your discretion. Taxi fares are rounded up by not more than 10 per cent.

Waiters and taxi drivers in **Hungary** expect a 10–15 per cent tip.

In **Slovakia**, a tip of around 10 per cent is usual in restaurants and for taxi drivers.

Even if a service charge is included, waiters often leave a space for an extra tip on credit card vouchers, and leave the total blank. Be sure to fill these in.

Toilets

Public facilities are generally clean. If there is an attendant, leave a small tip. If you use the toilets in a bar or café, it is customary to buy at least a drink there.

Voltage

220–240V AC, 50 Hz. Plugs are mainly of the two round pin type.

Water

Tap water may taste chlorinated. A wide choice of mineral waters, carbonated and still, is available.

On deck in time to capture the Walhalla monument.

hemis.fr/

LANDMARKS AT A GLANCE

The following table lists the landmarks on the left and right banks of the Danube, shown graphically on the fold-out map "Landmarks left and right".

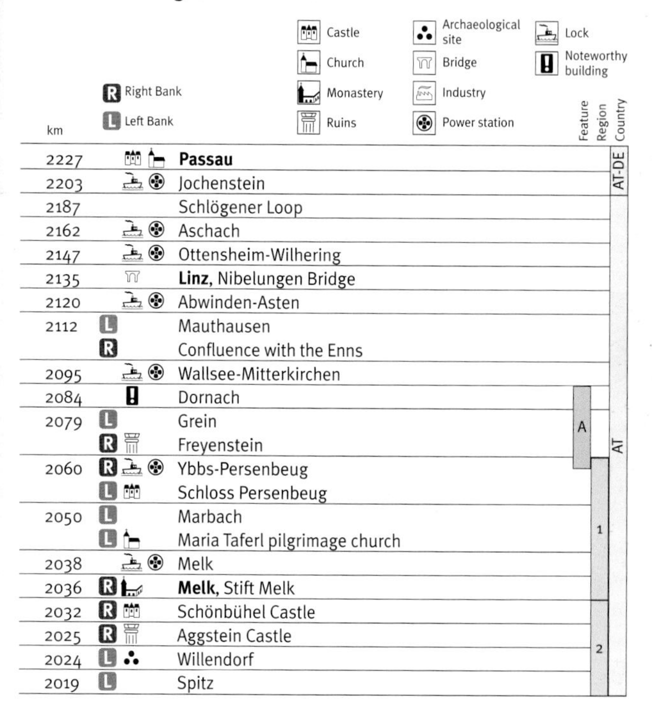

km	Bank	Feature	Name	Region	Country
2227		Castle, Church	**Passau**		AT-DE
2203		Lock, Power station	Jochenstein		AT-DE
2187			Schlögener Loop		AT
2162		Lock, Power station	Aschach		AT
2147		Lock, Power station	Ottensheim-Wilhering		AT
2135		Bridge	**Linz**, Nibelungen Bridge		AT
2120		Lock, Power station	Abwinden-Asten		AT
2112	L		Mauthausen		AT
	R		Confluence with the Enns		AT
2095		Lock, Power station	Wallsee-Mitterkirchen		AT
2084		Noteworthy building	Dornach	A	AT
2079	L		Grein	A	AT
	R	Ruins	Freyenstein	A	AT
2060	R	Lock, Power station	Ybbs-Persenbeug	1	AT
	L	Castle	Schloss Persenbeug	1	AT
2050	L		Marbach	1	AT
	L	Church	Maria Taferl pilgrimage church	1	AT
2038		Lock, Power station	Melk	1	AT
2036	R	Monastery	**Melk**, Stift Melk	1	AT
2032	R	Castle	Schönbühel Castle	2	AT
2025	R	Ruins	Aggstein Castle	2	AT
2024	L	Archaeological site	Willendorf	2	AT
2019	L		Spitz	2	AT

A. Strudengau, narrowing of the Danube Valley

1. Nibelungengau
2. Wachau

km	Bank	Landmark	Region	Country
2019	L	Burg Hinterhaus	2	AT
2013	L	Weissenkirchen	2	AT
2009	L	**Dürnstein**	2	AT
	L	Prison of Richard the Lionheart	2	AT
2002	R	Stift Göttweig, 5km south of the river	3	AT
	L	**Krems**	3	AT
	L	Gozzoburg, several churches	3	AT
1980		Altenwörth	3	AT
1977	R	Zwentendorf nuclear power station (abandoned)	3	AT
1963	R	Tulln	3	AT
1949		Greifenstein		AT
1943	L	Korneuburg, DDSG shipyard		AT
1939	R	Klosterneuburg		AT
1934		**Vienna**		AT
	R	Danube Canal to Vienna's Innenstadt		AT
1932	R	Hochhaus Millennium Tower		AT
1929	L	UNO-City		AT
1928		Reichsbrücke		AT
1921		Wien-Freudenau	4	AT
1890	R	Roman settlement of Carnuntum	4	AT
1884	R	Hainburg	4	AT
	R	Castle on the Braunsberg	4	AT
1880	L	Confluence with the Morava	4	SK-AT
	L	Devín Castle		SK-AT
1870	L	Bratislava Castle		SK
1869	L	**Bratislava**		SK
1866	L	Branch-off Little Danube/Malý Dunaj		SK
1853	R	(Lock and) branch-off main arm of Danube and Mosoni Duna	B	SK
		Danubiana Art Museum	B	SK
1821		Gabčikovo	B	SK
	R	Lock in Gabčikovo Canal at canal km 10	B	SK
1811	L	Confl. Gabčikovo Canal and main Danube branch	B	SK
1768	L	Komárno fortress		HU-SK
	R	Komárom fortress		HU-SK
1766	L	Confluence with the Váh		HU-SK
1719	L	Stúrovo		HU-SK

B. Gabčikovo Canal, 38.5 km long

2. Wachau

3. Tulln Basin

4. Donau-Auen National Park

km	Bank	Name		
1718	R	**Esztergom**	5	HU-SK
	R	Esztergom Basilica		
1719		Maria-Valeria Bridge		
1708	L	Confluence with the Ipoly		HU
1695	R	**Visegrád**		
1667	R	Confluence of Szentendre-Danube		
		Szentendre	C	
1680	L	**Vác**		
1663	L	Church by Imre Makovecs in Göd		
1657	R	Southern tip of Szentendre Island		
1655	R	Roman city of Aquincum		
1648	R	**Budapest**, Matthias Church		
	L	Parliament Buildings		
1647		Chain Bridge		
1580	R	Roman army base of Intercisa		
1578	R	Dunaújváros industrial city		
1531	R	Paks		
1526	R	Atomic power station Paks		
1516	L	**Kalocsa**, 5 km from the river		
1499		Motorway bridge		
1497	R	Confluence with the Sió from Balaton	D	
1480		Rail and road bridge		
1479	L	Baja, port	6	
1447	R	**Mohács**, port		
1433	R	Hungarian-Croatian frontier		

C. Szentendre-Danube

D. Gemenc Nature Reserve

5. Danube Bend

6. Duna-Drava National Park

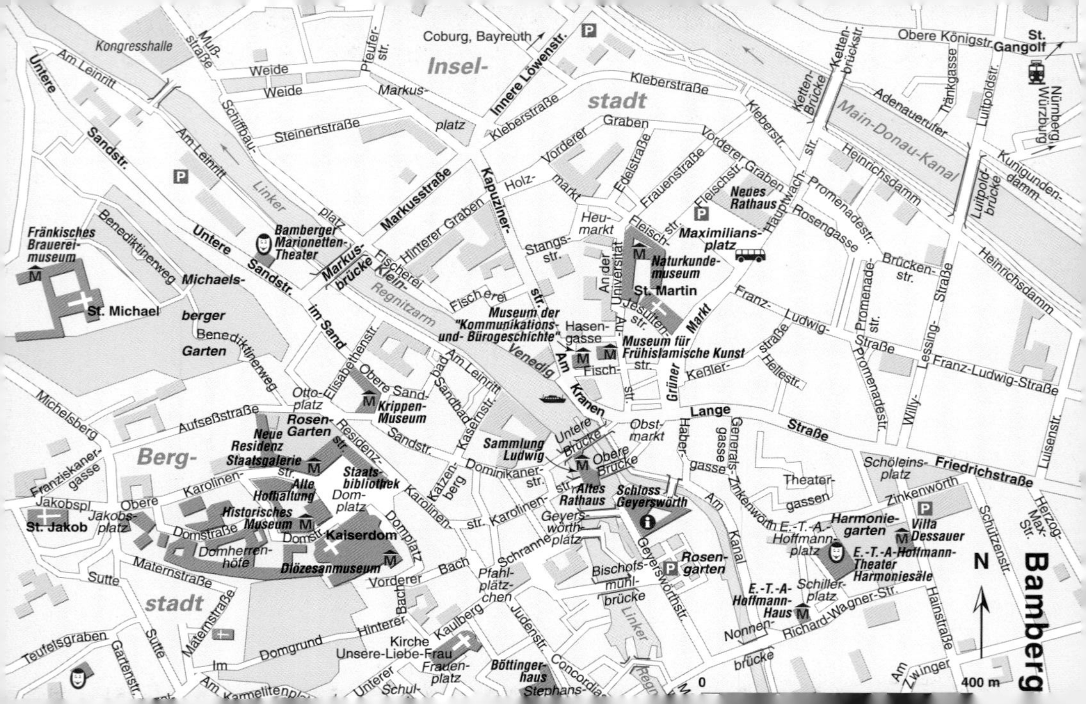

Bamberg
N
400 m
0
Nürnberg, Würzburg
Coburg, Bayreuth
Main-Donau-Kanal
Regnitzarm
Linker Regnitzarm
Insel-stadt
Berg-stadt
Neues Rathaus
Maximiliansplatz
Grüner Markt
Naturkundemuseum
St. Martin
Museum für Frühislamische Kunst
Museum der "Kommunikations- und Bürogeschichte"
Am Kranen
Klein-Venedig
Altes Rathaus
Schloss Geyerswörth
Rosengarten
Harmoniegarten
E.-T.-A-Hoffmann-Theater
Harmoniesäle
Villa Dessauer
E.-T.-A-Hoffmann-Haus
E.-T.-A.-Hoffmann-platz
Schillerplatz
Sammlung Ludwig
Krippen-Museum
Bamberger Marionetten-Theater
Staatsbibliothek
Kaiserdom
Diözesanmuseum
Alte Hofhaltung
Historisches Museum
Domherrenhöfe
Neue Residenz
Staatsgalerie
Rosen-Garten
Böttingerhaus
Kirche Unsere-Liebe-Frau
Michaelsberger Garten
Benediktinerweg
St. Michael
Fränkisches Brauereimuseum
St. Jakob
Jakobsplatz
Kongresshalle
St. Gangolf
Lange Straße
Friedrichstraße
Kapuziner-str.
Markusstraße
Innere Löwenstr.
Untere Sandstr.
Obere Sandstr.
Dominikanerstr.
Karolinenstr.
Domplatz
Obere Brücke
Untere Brücke
Kettenbrücke
Luitpoldbrücke
Markusbrücke
Nonnenbrücke
Bischofsmühlbrücke
Franz-Ludwig-Straße
Willy-Lessing-Straße
Promenadestr.
Heinrichsdamm
Kunigundendamm
Luitpoldstr.
Hainstraße
Schützenstr.
Herzog-Max-Str.
Luisenstr.
Kleberstraße
Hauptwachstr.
Obstmarkt
Heumarkt
Holzmarkt
Generalsgasse
Habergasse
Zinkenwörth
Am Kanal
Geyerswörthstr.
Geyerswörthplatz
Judenstr.
Concordiastr.
Pfahlplätzchen
Katzenberg
Sandbad
Am Leinritt
Richard-Wagner-Str.
Domgrund
Maternstraße
Sutte
Gartenstr.
Teufelsgraben
Michelsberg
Aufseßstraße
Elisabethenstr.
Weide
Mußstraße
Schiffbauplatz
Steinertstraße
Markusplatz
Pfeuferstr.
Obere Königstr.
Adenauerufer
Tränkgasse

Bratislava
Main Railway Station
Transport Museum
Sts Cyril and Methodius
Summer Archbishop´s Palace (Government Office)
Police Museum
Grassalkovich Palace
Stare mesto
St John of Matha and Felix of Valois
St Michael´s Gate
Franciscan Church
Hummel Museum
Jesuit Church
Mirbach Palace
Primate´s Palace
Old Town Hall
Church of the Poor Clares
Museum of Folk Music
Museum of Jewish Culture
House of the Good Shepherd
Pálffy Palace
Academia Istropolitana
Decorative Arts Museum
Bratislava Castle
St Martin Cathedral
Slovak National Theatre
Reduta Palace
Slovak National Gallery
Slovak National Museum
Church of St Elizabeth
Medická záhrada
Nám. slobody
Nám. SNP
Hurbanovo nám.
Hviezdoslavovo nám.
Kollárovo nám.
Nám. 1. mája
Hodžovo nám.
Rázusovo nábrežie
Fajnorovo nábr.
Nový most
Starý most
Danube (Dunaj)
0
800 m
N

Central Budapest

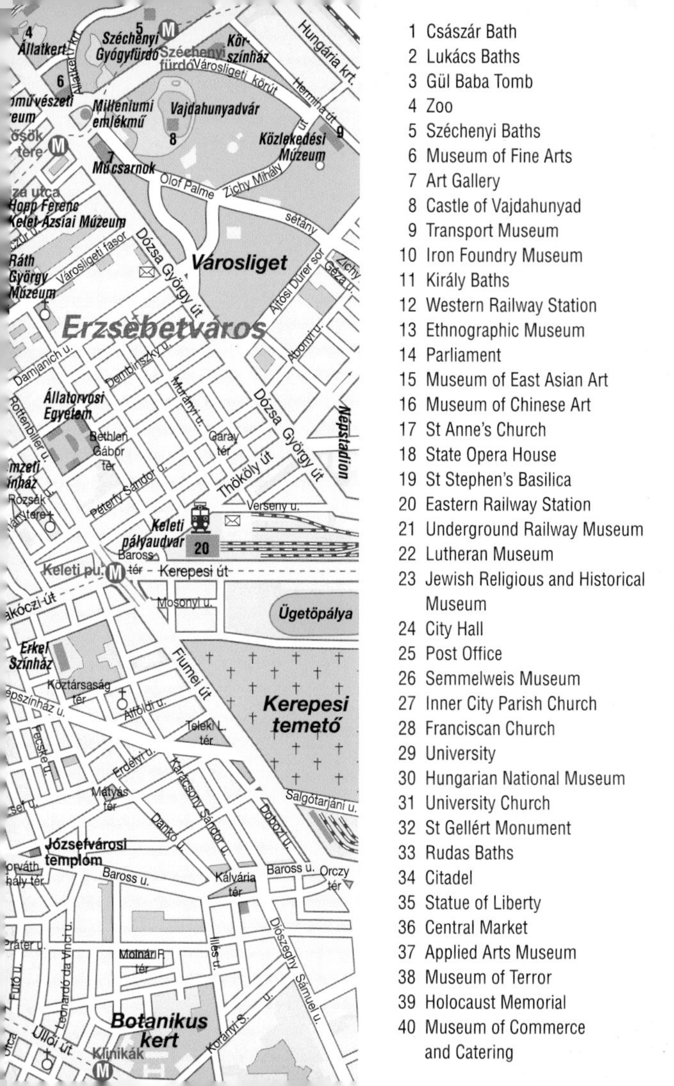

1 Császár Bath
2 Lukács Baths
3 Gül Baba Tomb
4 Zoo
5 Széchenyi Baths
6 Museum of Fine Arts
7 Art Gallery
8 Castle of Vajdahunyad
9 Transport Museum
10 Iron Foundry Museum
11 Király Baths
12 Western Railway Station
13 Ethnographic Museum
14 Parliament
15 Museum of East Asian Art
16 Museum of Chinese Art
17 St Anne's Church
18 State Opera House
19 St Stephen's Basilica
20 Eastern Railway Station
21 Underground Railway Museum
22 Lutheran Museum
23 Jewish Religious and Historical Museum
24 City Hall
25 Post Office
26 Semmelweis Museum
27 Inner City Parish Church
28 Franciscan Church
29 University
30 Hungarian National Museum
31 University Church
32 St Gellért Monument
33 Rudas Baths
34 Citadel
35 Statue of Liberty
36 Central Market
37 Applied Arts Museum
38 Museum of Terror
39 Holocaust Memorial
40 Museum of Commerce and Catering

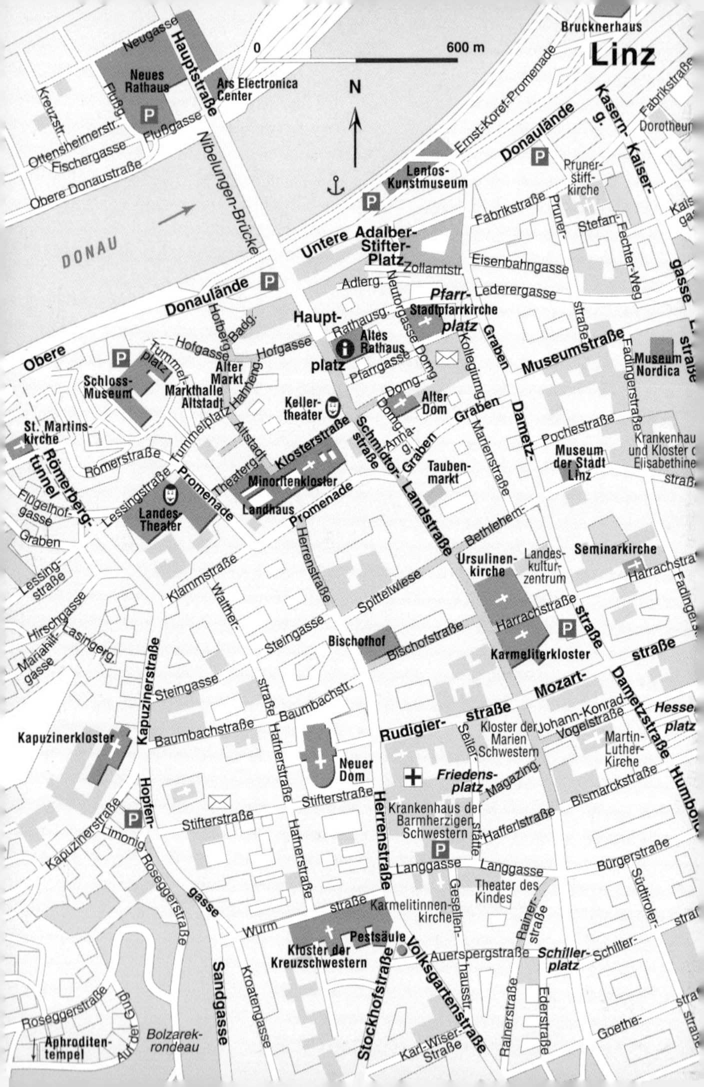

Linz
Brucknerhaus
0
600 m
N
DONAU
Neues Rathaus
Ars Electronica Center
Hauptstraße
Nibelungen-Brücke
Neugasse
Flußgasse
Ottensheimerstr.
Fischergasse
Obere Donaustraße
Kreuzstr.
Lentos-Kunstmuseum
Ernst-Koref-Promenade
Donaulände
Untere
Adalbert-Stifter-Platz
Zollamtstr.
Fabrikstraße
Eisenbahngasse
Lederergasse
Pruner-stift-kirche
Stefan-Fechter-Weg
Kasern-g.
Kaiser-gasse
Dorotheum
Obere
Schloss-Museum
Tummelplatz
Hofgasse
Hofberg
Badg.
Alter Markt
Markthalle Altstadt
Haupt-platz
Rathausg.
Altes Rathaus
Pfarrgasse
Adlerg.
Neutorgasse
Domg.
Stadtpfarrkirche
Pfarr-platz
Kollegiumg.
Graben
Museumstraße
Museum Nordica
Fadingerstraße
Keller-theater
Alter Dom
Anna-g.
Hahneng.
Altstadt
St. Martins-kirche
Römerberg-tunnel
Römerstraße
Klosterstraße
Minoritenkloster
Landhaus
Promenade
Theaterg.
Lessingstraße
Landes-Theater
Schmidtor-straße
Landstraße
Taubenmarkt
Marienstraße
Dametz-straße
Pochestraße
Museum der Stadt Linz
Krankenhaus und Kloster d. Elisabethinen
Bethlehem-
Flügelhof-gasse
Graben
Lessing-straße
Klammstraße
Walther-
Herrenstraße
Spittelwiese
Ursulinen-kirche
Landes-kultur-zentrum
Seminarkirche
Harrachstraße
Karmeliterkloster
Bischofhof
Bischofstraße
Steingasse
Hirschgasse
Lasingerg.
Mariahilf-gasse
Kapuzinerstraße
Mozart-straße
Rudigier-straße
Dametzstraße
Hessen-platz
Johann-Konrad-Vogelstraße
Kloster der Marien Schwestern
Martin-Luther-Kirche
Seiler-stätte
Baumbachstr.
Baumbachstraße
Hafnerstraße
Kapuzinerkloster
Neuer Dom
Friedens-platz
Magazing.
Bismarckstraße
Humboldt-
Stifterstraße
Krankenhaus der Barmherzigen Schwestern
Hafferlstraße
Hopfen-gasse
Limonig.
Roseggerstraße
Langgasse
Bürgerstraße
Südtiroler-straße
Theater des Kindes
Karmelitinnen-kirche
Gesellen-hausstr.
Rainerstraße
Wurmstraße
Pestsäule
Kloster der Kreuzschwestern
Volksgartenstraße
Auerspergstraße
Schiller-platz
Schillerstraße
Stockhofstraße
Sandgasse
Kroatengasse
Ederstraße
Goethestraße
Karl-Wiser-Straße
Aphroditen-tempel
Auf der Gugl
Bolzarek-rondeau

Main-Danube Canal
CZECH REPUBLIC
PRAGUE
KEY
Motorway
Highway
Secondary road
Railway
Frontier
International airport
Castle
Ruins
Church
GERMANY
AUSTRIA
Schweinfurt
Hassfurt
Main
Weißer Main
Roter Main
Veitshöchheim
Volkach
Würzburg
Schloss Eremitage
Bayreuth
Bamberg
Schloss Pommersfelden
Forchheim
Erlangen
Randersacker
Kitzingen
Ochsenfurt
Tauber
Main-Donau
Pegnitz
Fürth
Nürnberg
Rothenburg ob der Tauber
Amberg
Weiden
Plzeň
Schwandorf
Neumarkt
Regen
Cham
Berching
Hilpoltstein
Regensburg
Walhalla
Weißenburg
Wörnitz
Altmühl
Kanal
Riedenburg
Kelheim
Straubing
Deggendorf
Donaudurchbruch
Weltenburg
Plattling
Český Krumlov
Aalen
Donau
Neuburg an der Donau
Ingolstadt
Donauwörth
Dillingen
Ilz
Passau
Isar
Vils
Vilshofen
Schloss Ortenburg
Ulm
Günzburg
Neu-Ulm
Stuttgart
Augsburg
Landshut
Mühldorf
Linz
Inn
Leonding
Wels
Steyr
Braunau
München
Lech
Illertissen
Vaterstetten
Salzach
Landsberg
Starnberg
Gmunden
Memmingen
Kaufbeuren
Weilheim
Starnberger See
Rosenheim
Chiemsee
Salzburg
Attersee
Traunsee
Innsbruck
Bad Ischl

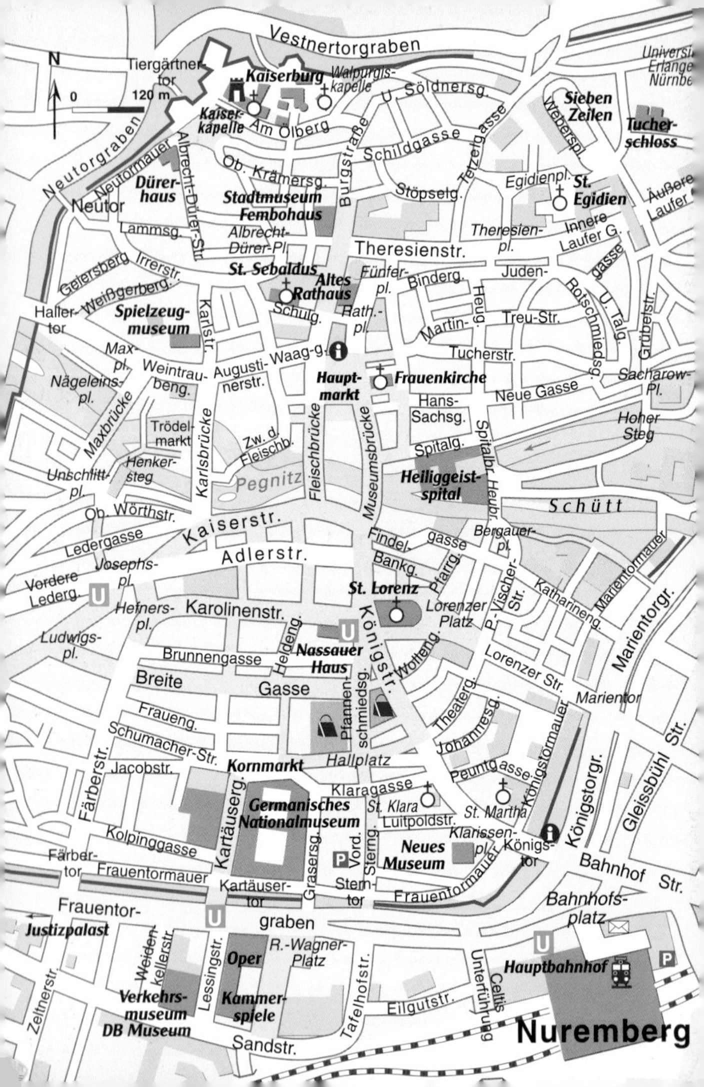

Nuremberg
N
0
120 m
Vestnertorgraben
Tiergärtnertor
Kaiserburg
Walpurgiskapelle
U. Söldnersg.
Kaiserkapelle
Am Ölberg
Schildgasse
Tetzelgasse
Sieben Zeilen
Tucherschloss
Webersp.
Universität Erlangen-Nürnberg
Neutorgraben
Neutormauer
Albrecht-Dürer-Str.
Dürerhaus
Ob. Krämersg.
Burgstraße
Stöpselg.
Egidienpl.
St. Egidien
Äußere Laufer G.
Neutor
Stadtmuseum Fembohaus
Lammsg.
Albrecht-Dürer-Pl.
Theresienpl.
Innere Laufer G.
Theresienstr.
Irrerstr.
Geiersberg
Weißgerberg.
St. Sebaldus
Altes Rathaus
Fünferpl.
Binderg.
Judengasse
Hallertor
Spielzeugmuseum
Karlstr.
Schulg.
Rath.-pl.
Heug.
Treu-Str.
Rotschmiedsg.
U. Talg.
Grübelstr.
Maxpl.
Weintraubeng.
Augustinerstr.
Waag-g.
Martin-
Tucherstr.
Nägeleinspl.
Hauptmarkt
Frauenkirche
Neue Gasse
Sacharow-Pl.
Maxbrücke
Trödelmarkt
Karlsbrücke
Zw. d. Fleischb.
Fleischbrücke
Museumsbrücke
Hans-Sachsg.
Spitalg.
Spitalbr.
Hohen Steg
Henkersteg
Unschlittpl.
Pegnitz
Heiliggeistspital
Heubr.
Schütt
Ob. Wörthstr.
Kaiserstr.
Ledergasse
Findelgasse
Bergauerpl.
Adlerstr.
Bankg.
Pfarrg.
Josephspl.
Vordere Lederg.
St. Lorenz
P.-Vischer-Str.
Katharineng.
Marientormauer
Marientorgr.
Hefnerspl.
Karolinenstr.
Lorenzer Platz
Königstr.
Ludwigspl.
Heldeng.
Nassauer Haus
Wolfeng.
Brunnengasse
Lorenzer Str.
Breite Gasse
Pfannenschmiedsg.
Theaterg.
Marientor
Johannesg.
Fraueng.
Schumacher-Str.
Königstormauer
Gleissbühl Str.
Jacobstr.
Kornmarkt
Hallplatz
Peuntgasse
Königstorgr.
Färberstr.
Klaragasse
St. Klara
St. Martha
Germanisches Nationalmuseum
Luitpoldstr.
Kartäuserg.
Grasersg.
Vord. Sterng.
Klarissenpl.
Kolpinggasse
Neues Museum
Königstor
Färbertor
Frauentormauer
Bahnhof Str.
Kartäusertor
Sterntor
Frauentor-graben
Bahnhofsplatz
Justizpalast
Weidenkellerstr.
Lessingstr.
Oper
R.-Wagner-Platz
Tafelhofstr.
Unterführung
Celtis
Hauptbahnhof
Verkehrsmuseum DB Museum
Kammerspiele
Eilgutstr.
Zeltnerstr.
Sandstr.

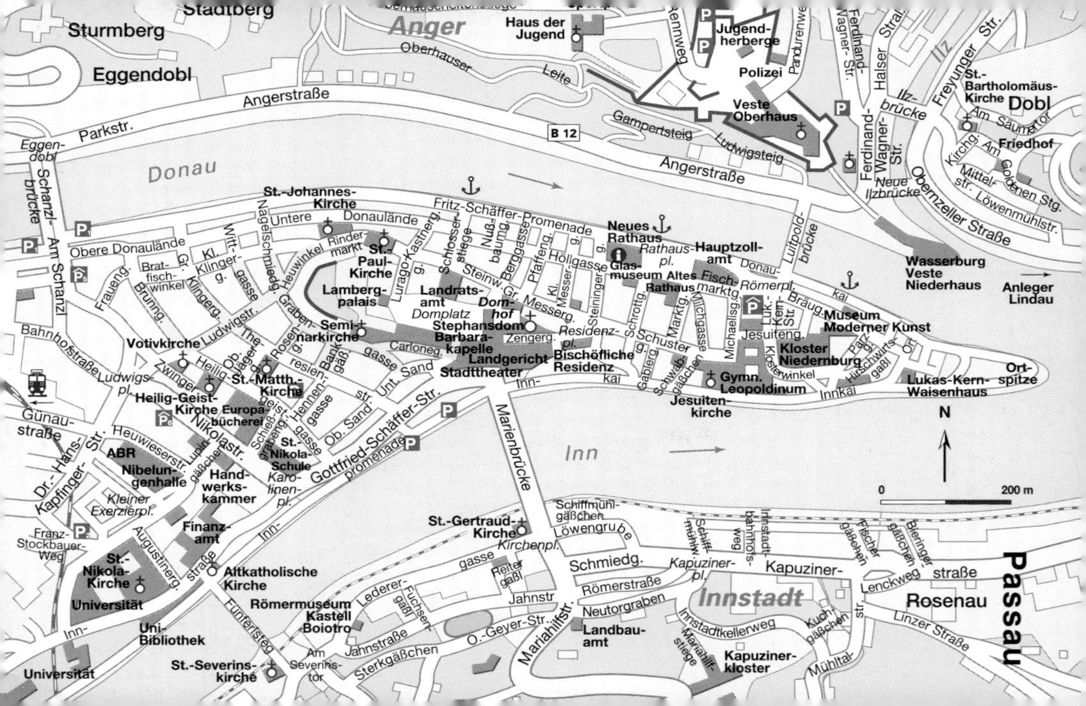
Passau
Rosenau
Innstadt
Inn
Donau
Ilz
Anger
Eggendobl
Sturmberg
Staatberg
Dobl
Ort-spitze
Lukas-Kern-Waisenhaus
Wasserburg Veste Niederhaus
Anleger Lindau
Museum Moderner Kunst
Kloster Niedernburg
Gymn. Leopoldinum
Jesuitenkirche
Hauptzollamt
Neues Rathaus
Glasmuseum Altes Rathaus
Bischöfliche Residenz
Landgericht
Stadttheater
Stephansdom
Dom-hof
Barbara-kapelle
Landratsamt
Dompl atz
St.-Paul-Kirche
Lambergpalais
Seminarkirche
St.-Johannes-Kirche
St.-Matth.-Kirche
Europabücherei
Heilig-Geist-Kirche
Votivkirche
St.-Nikola-Schule
Handwerkskammer
Finanzamt
ABR
Nibelungenhalle
St.-Nikola-Kirche
Universität
Uni-Bibliothek
Altkatholische Kirche
Römermuseum Kastell Boiotro
St.-Severins-kirche
St.-Gertraud-Kirche
Landbauamt
Kapuzinerkloster
Veste Oberhaus
Polizei
Jugendherberge
Haus der Jugend
St.-Bartholomäus-Kirche
Friedhof
Marienbrücke
Luitpoldbrücke
Schanzlbrücke
Ilzbrücke
Neue Ilzbrücke
Angerstraße
Obernzeller Straße
Freyunger Str.
Halser Straße
Ferdinand-Wagner-Str.
Ludwigsteig
Gampertsteig
Rennweg
Panduren weg
Leite
Oberhauser
B 12
Parkstr.
Eggendobl
Am Schanzl
Bahnhofstraße
Ludwigspl.
Ludwigstr.
Güna ustraße
Dr.-Hans-Kapfinger-Str.
Heuwieserstr.
Nikolastr.
Gottfried-Schäffer-Promenade
Unt. Sandstr.
Ob. Sand
Innkai
Inn-kai
Fritz-Schäffer-Promenade
Untere Donaulände
Obere Donaulände
Donaukai
Rathauspl.
Fischmarkt
Römerpl.
Michaelisg.
Milchgasse
Marktg.
Schrottg.
Schusterg.
Gablerg.
Schwabgäßchen
Residenzpl.
Zengerg.
Steiningerg.
Höllgasse
Kl. Messerg.
Gr. Messerg.
Pfaffeng.
Berggasse
Nußbaumg.
Steinw.
Schlossersteige
Luragog.
Kastnerg.
Rindermarkt
Heuwinkel
Nagelschmiedg.
Grabeng.
Rosenau g.
Bankgäßl
Sandgasse
Carloneg.
Theresienstr.
Hennengasse
Geistgasse
Schiebgasse
Karolinenpl.
Ob. Jägerg.
Heilig-Geist-g.
Zwinger
Wittgasse
Kl. Klingerg.
Gr. Klingerg.
Klingerg.
Bratfischwinkel
Brunng.
Fraueng.
Jesuiteng.
Lukas-Kern-Str.
Bräug.
Klosterwinkel
Hirschwirtsg.
Ort
Pfaffeng.
Am Säumertor
Am Goldenen Stg.
Mittelstr.
Kirchg.
Löwenmühlstr.
Bieringergäßchen
Fischergäßchen
Lenckweg
Bieringer straße
Linzer Straße
Kapuzinerstr.
Innstadtbahnhofsweg
Schiffmühlw.
Kapuzinerpl.
Kuchlgäßchen
Mühltal
Innstadtkellerweg
Mariahilfstiege
Schiffmühlgäßchen
Löwengrube
Schmiedg.
Römerstraße
Neutorgraben
Mariahilfstr.
Kirchenpl.
Reitergäßl
Jahnstr.
O.-Geyer-Str.
Gassen
Ledererg.
Fuchsengäßl
Jahnstraße
Sterkgäßchen
Am Severinstor
Fünferlsteg
Innstraße
Augustinerg.
Kleiner Exerzierpl.
Franz-Stockbauer-Weg
Lupingäßchen
0
200 m
N

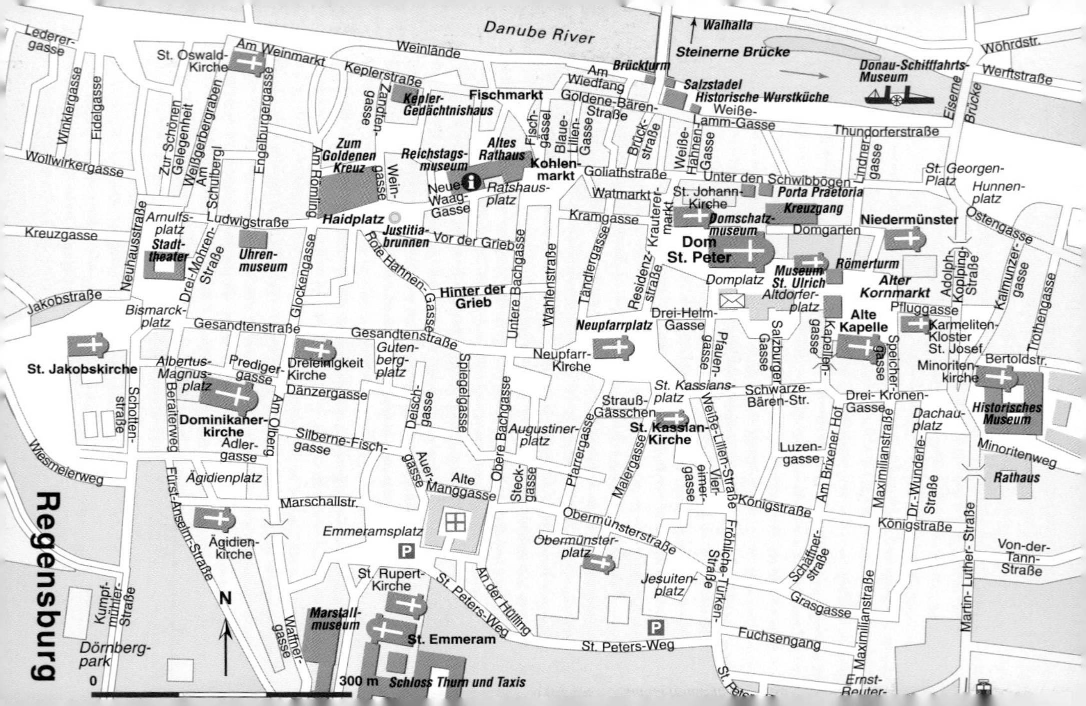

Danube River
Walhalla
Steinerne Brücke
Donau-Schifffahrts-Museum
Wöhrdstr.
Werftstraße
Eiserne Brücke
Lederergasse
Am Weinmarkt
St. Oswald-Kirche
Weinlände
Keplerstraße
Brückturm
Am Wiedfang
Salzstadel
Historische Wurstküche
Weiße-Lamm-Gasse
Thundorferstraße
Winklergasse
Fidelgasse
Zur Schönen Gelegenheit
Weißgerbergraben
Am Schulbergl
Engelburgergasse
Zandtengasse
Kepler-Gedächtnishaus
Fischmarkt
Goldene-Bären-Straße
Brückstraße
Weiße-Hahnen-Gasse
Lindnergasse
St. Georgen-Platz
Hunnenplatz
Wollwirkergasse
Zum Goldenen Kreuz
Am Römling
Weingasse
Reichstagsmuseum
Altes Rathaus
Fischgässel
Blaue-Lilien-Gasse
Kohlenmarkt
Goliathstraße
Unter den Schwibbögen
Neue-Waag-Gasse
Rathausplatz
Watmarkt
St. Johann-Kirche
Porta Praetoria
Kreuzgang
Niedermünster
Ostengasse
Arnulfsplatz
Ludwigstraße
Haidplatz
Justitiabrunnen
Vor der Grieb
Kramgasse
Krauterermarkt
Domschatzmuseum
Domgarten
Kreuzgasse
Neuhausstraße
Stadttheater
Drei-Mohren-Straße
Uhrenmuseum
Glockengasse
Rote-Hahnen-Gasse
Untere Bachgasse
Wahlenstraße
Tändlergasse
Residenzstraße
Dom St. Peter
Museum St. Ulrich
Römerturm
Adolph-Kolping-Straße
Kalmunzergasse
Trothengasse
Jakobstraße
Bismarckplatz
Hinter der Grieb
Domplatz
Altdorferplatz
Alter Kornmarkt
Pfluggasse
Gesandtenstraße
Neupfarrplatz
Drei-Helm-Gasse
Alte Kapelle
Karmeliten-Kloster St. Josef
St. Jakobskirche
Albertus-Magnus-platz
Predigergasse
Dreieinigkeit Kirche
Gutenbergplatz
Spiegelgasse
Neupfarr-Kirche
Pfauengasse
Salzburger Gasse
Kapellengasse
Speichergasse
Bertoldstr.
Minoritenkirche
Schottenstraße
Beraiterweg
Dominikanerkirche
Am Ölberg
Dänzergasse
Deischgasse
St. Kassiansplatz
Schwarze-Bären-Str.
Drei-Kronen-Gasse
Historisches Museum
Dachauplatz
Adlergasse
Silberne-Fischgasse
Obere Bachgasse
Augustinerplatz
Strauß-Gässchen
St. Kassian-Kirche
Luzengasse
Am Brixener Hof
Wiesmeierweg
Ägidienplatz
Fürst-Anselm-Straße
Auergasse
Alte Manggasse
Steckgasse
Pfarrergasse
Malergasse
Viereimergasse
Weiße-Lilien-Straße
Maximilianstraße
Dr.-Wunderle-Straße
Minoritenweg
Rathaus
Marschallstr.
Königstraße
Regensburg
Ägidienkirche
Emmeramsplatz
Obermünsterstraße
Obermünsterplatz
Von-der-Tann-Straße
Martin-Luther-Straße
St. Rupert-Kirche
St. Peters-Weg
An der Hülling
Jesuitenplatz
Fröhliche-Türken-Straße
Schäffnerstraße
Grasgasse
Kumpfmühler-Straße
N
Waffnergasse
Marstallmuseum
St. Emmeram
Fuchsengang
Dörnbergpark
0
300 m
Schloss Thurn und Taxis
St. Peters-Weg
Ernst-Reuter-

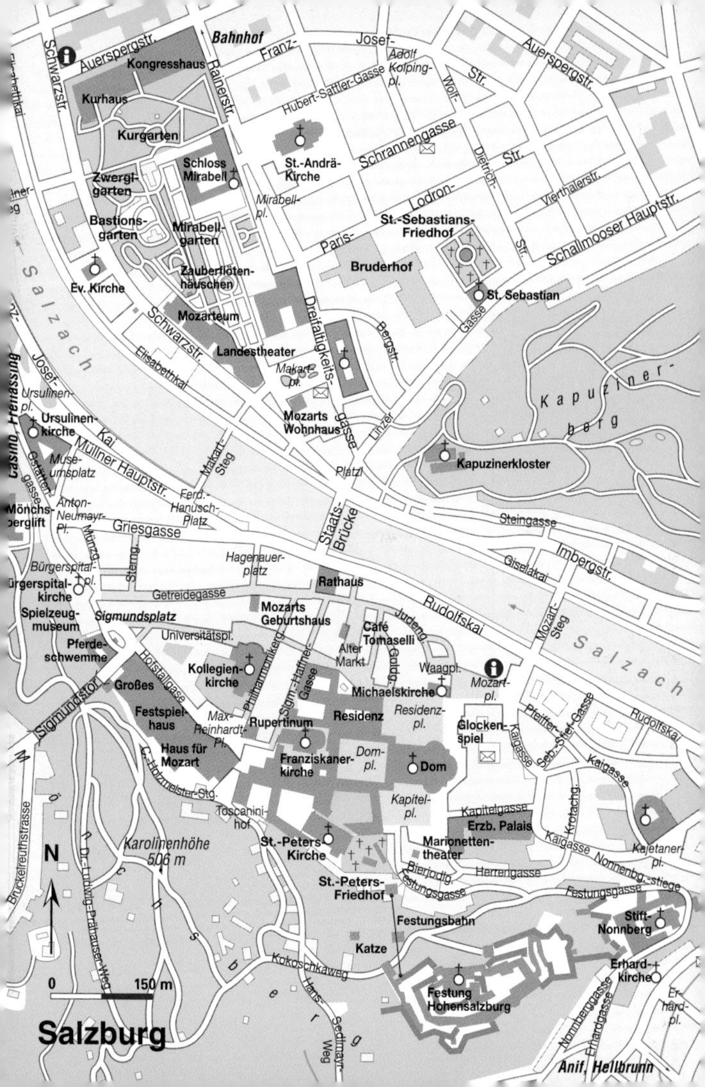
Salzburg
Bahnhof
Kongresshaus
Kurhaus
Kurgarten
Schloss Mirabell
Zwergl-garten
Bastions-garten
Mirabell-garten
Zauberflöten-häuschen
Mozarteum
Landestheater
Ev. Kirche
St.-Andrä-Kirche
Mirabell-pl.
St.-Sebastians-Friedhof
Bruderhof
St. Sebastian
Kapuzinerberg
Kapuzinerkloster
Makart-pl.
Mozarts Wohnhaus
Ursulinen-pl.
Ursulinen-kirche
Museumsplatz
Mönchsberglift
Anton-Neumayr-Pl.
Ferd.-Hanusch-Platz
Platzl
Staats-Brücke
Hagenauer-platz
Rathaus
Bürgerspital-pl.
Bürgerspital-kirche
Spielzeug-museum
Sigmundsplatz
Pferde-schwemme
Mozarts Geburtshaus
Café Tomaselli
Alter Markt
Universitätspl.
Kollegien-kirche
Großes Festspiel-haus
Haus für Mozart
Max-Reinhardt-Pl.
Rupertinum
Residenz
Residenz-pl.
Michaelskirche
Waagpl.
Mozart-pl.
Glocken-spiel
Franziskaner-kirche
Dom-pl.
Dom
Kapitel-pl.
Toscaninihof
Erzb. Palais
St.-Peters-Kirche
Marionetten-theater
St.-Peters-Friedhof
Festungsbahn
Katze
Karolinenhöhe 506 m
Mönchsberg
Festung Hohensalzburg
Stift-Nonnberg
Erhard-kirche
Erhard-pl.
Kajetaner-pl.
Anif, Hellbrunn
Casino, Freilassing
Salzach
Auerspergstr.
Schwarzstr.
Rainerstr.
Franz-Josef-Str.
Adolf Kolping-pl.
Hubert-Sattler-Gasse
Wolf-Dietrich-Str.
Schrannengasse
Paris-Lodron-Str.
Vierthalerstr.
Schallmooser Hauptstr.
Dreifaltigkeits-gasse
Bergstr.
Linzer Gasse
Elisabethkai
Makart-Steg
Müllner Hauptstr.
Josef-Kai
Gstättengasse
Griesgasse
Münzg.
Sterng.
Getreidegasse
Steingasse
Imbergstr.
Giselakai
Rudolfskai
Mozart-Steg
Judeng.
Goldg.
Hofstallgasse
Sigmundstor
Philharmonikerg.
Sigm.-Haffner-Gasse
Pfeiffer-Gasse
Seb.-Stief-Gasse
Kaigasse
Krotachg.
Kapitelgasse
Herrengasse
Bierjodlg.
Festungsgasse
Nonnbg.-stiege
Kokoschkaweg
Hans-Sedlmayr-Weg
Dr.-Ludwig-Prähauser-Weg
C.-Holzmeister-Stg.
Bruckelreuthstrasse
Nonnberggasse
Erhardgasse
N
0
150 m

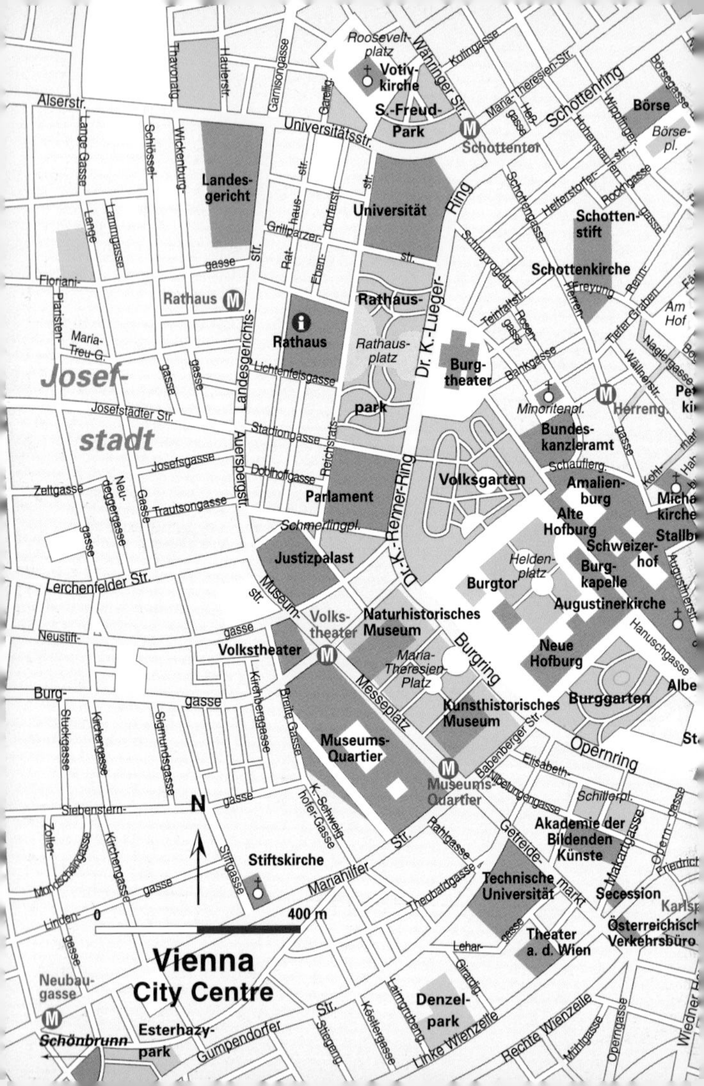

Vienna
City Centre
Votivkirche
Roosevelt-platz
S.-Freud-Park
Schottentor
Schottenring
Börse
Börse-pl.
Landesgericht
Universität
Schottenstift
Schottenkirche
Rathaus
Rathaus-park
Rathausplatz
Burgtheater
Josefstadt
Minoritenpl.
Herreng.
Bundeskanzleramt
Volksgarten
Amalienburg
Alte Hofburg
Schweizerhof
Parlament
Justizpalast
Heldenplatz
Burgtor
Burgkapelle
Augustinerkirche
Naturhistorisches Museum
Volkstheater
Neue Hofburg
Maria-Theresien-Platz
Burggarten
Kunsthistorisches Museum
MuseumsQuartier
Opernring
Schillerpl.
Akademie der Bildenden Künste
Stiftskirche
Technische Universität
Secession
Österreichische Verkehrsbüro
Theater a. d. Wien
Denzelpark
Esterhazypark
Neubaugasse
Schönbrunn
0
400 m
N

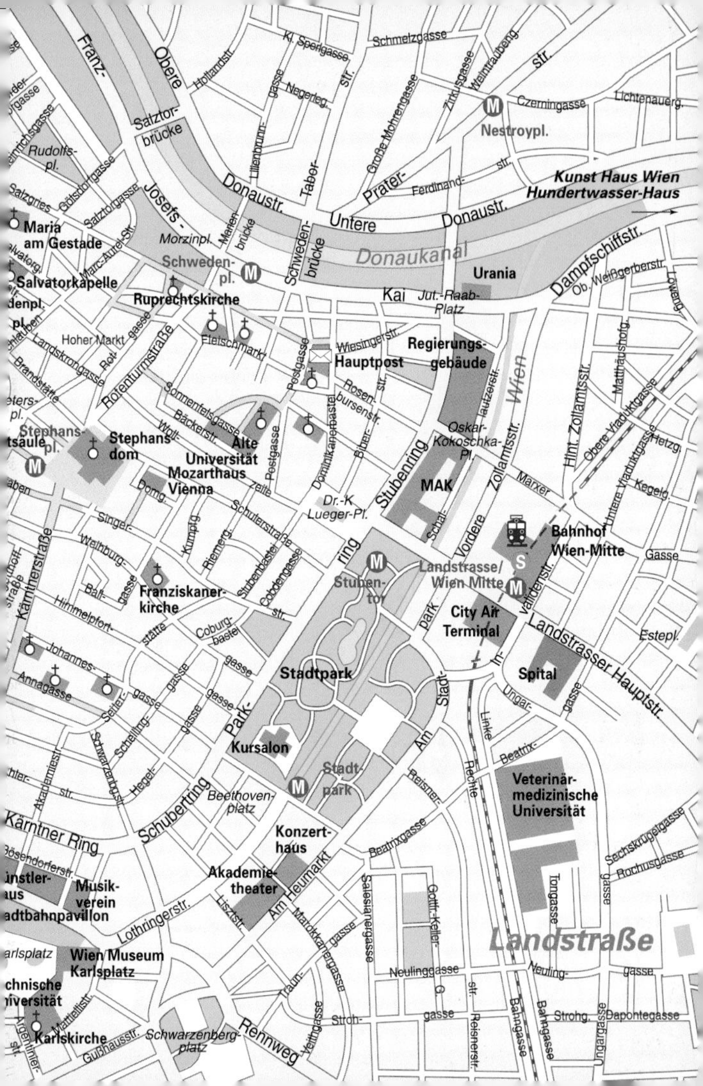

Franz-
Obere
Salztorbrücke
Kl. Sperlgasse
Schmelzgasse
Weintraubeng.
str.
Hollandstr.
Negerlg.
Große Mohrengasse
Zirkusgasse
Czerningasse
Lichtenauerg.
Nestroypl.
Rudolfspl.
Gölsdorfgasse
Salztorgasse
Josefs-
Donaustr.
Lilienbrunngasse
Taborstr.
Prater-
Ferdinand-str.
Kunst Haus Wien
Hundertwasser-Haus
Salzgries
Maria am Gestade
Marc-Aurel-Str.
Morzinpl.
Marienbrücke
Schwedenbrücke
Untere Donaustr.
Donaukanal
Dampfschiffstr.
Salvatorkapelle
Schwedenpl.
Kai
Jul.-Raab-Platz
Urania
Ob. Weißgerberstr.
Löweng.
Ruprechtskirche
Hoher Markt
Rotgasse
Fleischmarkt
Wiesingerstr.
Hauptpost
Postgasse
Regierungsgebäude
Landskrongasse
Brandstätte
Rotenturmstraße
Sonnenfelsgasse
Bäckerstr.
Rosenbursenstr.
Biberstr.
Dominikanerbastei
Oskar-Kokoschka-Pl.
Wien
Zollamtsstr.
Hint. Zollamtsstr.
Matthäushofg.
Obere Viaduktgasse
Stephanspl.
Stephansdom
Wollzeile
Alte Universität
Mozarthaus Vienna
Domg.
Schulerstraße
Dr.-K Lueger-Pl.
Stubenring
MAK
Marxer
Hetzg.
Kegelg.
Untere Viaduktgasse
Singerstr.
Kärntnerstraße
Weihburggasse
Kumpfg.
Riemerg.
Stubenbastei
Cobdengasse
Stubentor
Landstrasse/Wien Mitte
Schallautzerstr.
Vordere Zollamtsstr.
Bahnhof Wien-Mitte
Gasse
Ballgasse
Franziskanerkirche
Himmelpfortgasse
Seilerstätte
Coburgbastei
Parkring
Stadtpark
City Air Terminal
Invalidenstr.
Landstrasser Hauptstr.
Estepl.
Johannesgasse
Annagasse
Spital
Ungargasse
Schellinggasse
Kursalon
Am Stadtpark
Linke
Rechte
Beatrixgasse
Akademiestr.
Schwarzenbergstr.
Hegelgasse
Reisnerstr.
Veterinärmedizinische Universität
Beethovenplatz
Kärntner Ring
Schubertring
Konzerthaus
Sechskrügelgasse
Rochusgasse
Bösendorferstr.
Künstlerhaus
Musikverein
Akademietheater
Am Heumarkt
Salesianergasse
Gottfr.-Keller-G.
Tongasse
Stadtbahnpavillon
Lothringerstr.
Lisztstr.
Marokkanergasse
Landstraße
Karlsplatz
Wien Museum Karlsplatz
Traungasse
Neulinggasse
Technische Universität
Mattiellistr.
Karlskirche
Gußhausstr.
Schwarzenbergplatz
Rennweg
Veithgasse
Strohgasse
Reisnerstr.
Bahngasse
Strohg.
Dapontegasse
Ungargasse
Argentinierstr.

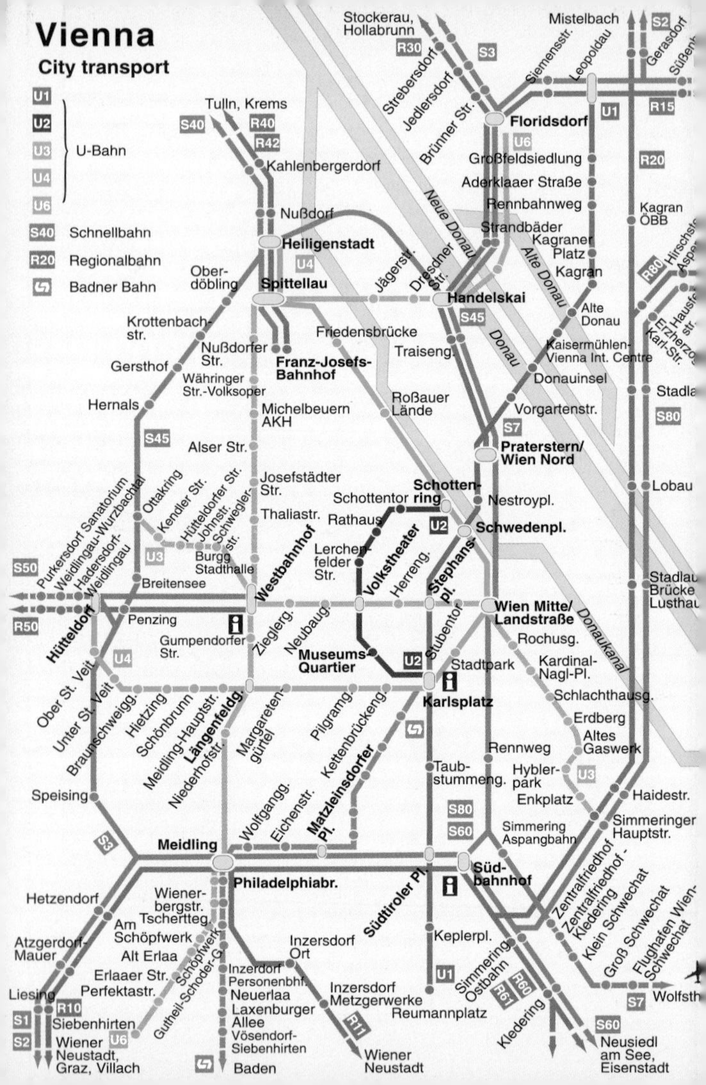

Vienna
City transport
U1
U2
U3
U4
U6
U-Bahn
S40 Schnellbahn
R20 Regionalbahn
Badner Bahn
Stockerau, Hollabrunn
Mistelbach
Tulln, Krems
Kahlenbergerdorf
Nußdorf
Heiligenstadt
Spittellau
Oberdöbling
Krottenbach-str.
Gersthof
Hernals
Nußdorfer Str.
Franz-Josefs-Bahnhof
Währinger Str.-Volksoper
Michelbeuern AKH
Alser Str.
Josefstädter Str.
Thaliastr.
Burgg. Stadthalle
Westbahnhof
Floridsdorf
Großfeldsiedlung
Aderklaaer Straße
Rennbahnweg
Strandbäder
Kagraner Platz
Kagran
Alte Donau
Kaisermühlen-Vienna Int. Centre
Donauinsel
Vorgartenstr.
Praterstern/Wien Nord
Nestroypl.
Schwedenpl.
Schottenring
Schottentor
Rathaus
Lerchenfelder Str.
Volkstheater
Herreng.
Stephanspl.
Wien Mitte/Landstraße
Rochusg.
Kardinal-Nagl-Pl.
Schlachthausg.
Erdberg
Altes Gaswerk
Hyblerpark
Enkplatz
Simmering Aspangbahn
Simmeringer Hauptstr.
Haidestr.
Handelskai
Friedensbrücke
Traiseng.
Roßauer Lände
Jägerstr.
Dresdner Str.
Neue Donau
Alte Donau
Donau
Donaukanal
Siemensstr.
Leopoldau
Strebersdorf
Jedlersdorf
Brünner Str.
Gerasdorf
Kagran ÖBB
Hirschstetten
Aspern
Hausfeldstr.
Erzherzog-Karl-Str.
Stadlau
Lobau
Stadlau Brücke Lusthaus
Purkersdorf Sanatorium
Weidlingau-Wurzbachtal
Hadersdorf-Weidlingau
Hütteldorf
Penzing
Breitensee
Ottakring
Kendler Str.
Hütteldorfer Str.
Johnstr.
Schweglerstr.
Gumpendorfer Str.
Zieglerg.
Neubaug.
Museums-Quartier
Stubentor
Stadtpark
Karlsplatz
Ober St. Veit
Unter St. Veit
Braunschweigg.
Hietzing
Schönbrunn
Meidling-Hauptstr.
Längenfeldg.
Niederhofstr.
Margaretengürtel
Pilgramg.
Kettenbrückeng.
Matzleinsdorfer Pl.
Taubstummeng.
Rennweg
Speising
Meidling
Wolfgangg.
Eichenstr.
Philadelphiabr.
Südtiroler Pl.
Südbahnhof
Hetzendorf
Wienerbergstr.
Am Schöpfwerk
Tscherttteg.
Alt Erlaa
Atzgerdorf-Mauer
Erlaaer Str.
Perfektastr.
Liesing
Siebenhirten
Schöpfwerk
Gutheil-Schoder-G.
Inzersdorf Ort
Inzerdorf Personenbhf.
Neuerlaa
Laxenburger Allee
Vösendorf-Siebenhirten
Baden
Inzersdorf Metzgerwerke
Reumannplatz
Keplerpl.
Simmering Ostbahn
Kledering
Wiener Neustadt
Wiener Neustadt, Graz, Villach
Zentralfriedhof
Zentralfriedhof-Kledering
Klein Schwechat
Groß Schwechat
Flughafen Wien-Schwechat
Wolfsthal
Neusiedl am See, Eisenstadt
S1
S2
S3
S7
S40
S45
S50
S60
S80
R10
R11
R15
R20
R30
R40
R42
R50
R60
R61
R80

General editor
Barbara Ender-Jones

Translation, editorial assistance
Jack Altman

Research, technical assistance
Elke Frey

Design
Karin Palazzolo

Layout
Karin Palazzolo
Luc Malherbe

Photo credits
p. 2: Corbis.com (pelicans);
Claude Huber (fisherman, horse show);
Wien Tourismus (Strauss)

Maps
JPM Publications,
Mathieu Germay
Jonathan Reymond

12, avenue William-Fraisse,
1006 Lausanne, Switzerland
information@jpmguides.com
http://www.jpmguides.com/

Printed in Germany
12176.00.12321
Edition 2012